GASTROPARESIS COOKBOOK

130+ Recipes To Alleviate Nausea, Pain, And Acid Reflux Without Compromising Taste.
You Can Live Your Best Life And Get Fast Relief From Gastroparesis By Eating Delicious
Foods

By Mamie A. Gutierrez

TABLE OF CONTENTS

Introduction

Gastroparesis is a medical condition that slows digestion by making it take longer for the stomach to empty. It is caused when the muscles in the stomach do not function properly, which leads to the condition. Patients with this condition often feel sick, throw up, have stomach pain, get bloated, and feel full after only a few bites of food.

Damage to the nerves that control the stomach muscles is what causes gastroparesis. This nerve damage can be the result of a number of different things, including diabetes, surgery, viral infections, or the use of certain medications. In some people, the reason why they have gastroparesis is a mystery.

Several tests, like upper endoscopy, gastric emptying studies, and manometry, can be used to figure out what's wrong. These tests measure the pressure inside the stomach and how well the muscles that make up the organ are working.

To treat gastroparesis, a patient may need to make changes to their diet, take medicine, or even have surgery. A registered dietitian can assist in the creation of a meal plan that is high in fiber and low in fat, as well as one that consists of meals that are both smaller and more frequent. A doctor can also give you medicine, such as prokinetic agents, which help speed up the stomach's contractions.

The majority of people who have gastroparesis can lead a life that is close to normal with the proper management and treatment of their condition. However, gastroparesis can be a chronic condition. If you have symptoms of gastroparesis, you need to see a doctor right away. This is because the condition can lead to problems like malnutrition, dehydration, and other digestive issues. If you are experiencing symptoms of gastroparesis, it is important to seek medical attention.

PART ONE: WHAT YOU NEED TO KNOW ABOUT GASTROPARESIS:

CHAPTER 1: WHAT IS GASTROPARESIS?

Gastroparesis is also called delayed gastric emptying. The term "gastric" refers to the stomach.

The stomach normally releases its contents into the small intestine in a measured fashion. When someone has Gastroparesis, their stomach empties at a much slower rate than usual because the muscle contractions (motility) that empty the stomach don't perform properly.

This condition can be diagnosed by long-term symptoms, such as a stomach that takes longer to empty when there is no blockage or obstruction. A test confirms sluggish gastric emptying.

More research has shown that this illness affects a large number of people and has a wide range of symptoms that vary in how often they show up and how bad they are.

CHAPTER 2: CAUSES OF GASTROPARESIS

Gastroparesis can have multiple causes. The majority of people who have Gastroparesis have idiopathic symptoms, which means that doctors haven't figured out what causes their condition. When talking about Gastroparesis, is the most prevalent form. When a sickness is labeled "idiopathic," it simply indicates that its cause is unknown. Idiopathic Gastroparesis accounts for roughly 30%-50% of all cases of Gastroparesis. Some patients have reported idiopathic gastroparesis symptoms after a viral illness. More research is needed to confirm whether or not the many proposed reasons for idiopathic Gastroparesis are, in fact, real causes or risk factors for developing GP.

Other possible causes of Gastroparesis include: Diabetes, Surgeries, Medications, Other illnesses, Cellular changes

Diabetes

Gastroparesis can develop secondary to a variety of medical issues. Although only a small fraction of people with diabetes develop Gastroparesis, long-term diabetes is the most commonly known cause of Gastroparesis.

A lack of insulin or an abnormal response to insulin characterizes diabetes mellitus. The pancreas secretes the hormone insulin, which controls blood sugar levels. This disorder results in blood sugar levels that are significantly higher than normal. People with diabetes are more prone to developing diabetic Gastroparesis when they experience delayed gastric emptying.

Diabetic Gastroparesis is found in about 25% of people with Gastroparesis. Both type 1 and type 2 diabetics are vulnerable to this condition. Symptoms of diabetic GP typically persist even after blood sugar levels have been brought under control. Comparable to the neuropathy seen in the feet of diabetics, diabetic GP happens when blood sugar levels get too high. Over time, nerve damage might occur if blood sugar levels aren't kept in check. The affected long nerves reach all the way down to the feet, making diabetic foot neuropathy a very serious condition. The nerves that supply the stomach and its lining are especially vulnerable to injury in diabetics with GP.

Viral Infections

The majority of cases are due to viruses. Viral gastroenteritis refers to infections of the gastrointestinal tract caused by viruses. This can be caused by any virus that affects the gastrointestinal tract, including COVID-19. Norovirus and rotavirus illnesses are two others that frequently strike young children. Patients with viral GP may experience symptom improvement months or even years after becoming ill.

Surgeries

Surgery that alters the stomach can cause GP. This may occur because of scar tissue growth in the stomach or because of nerve injury. When the vagus nerve has been hurt, it is often thought to be the cause of symptoms that a doctor would recognize. The brain's vagus nerve extends to the chest and belly, where it regulates vital organs like the heart, lungs, and esophagus.

Surgeries that cause some cases of GP include: Nissen fundoplication is a surgical procedure used to treat GERD and hiatus hernia.

The Surgical Removal of the Gallbladder (Colectomy) Gallbladder removal is a common surgery done on people who have pain in the upper right part of their abdomen or who have gallstones, which are small deposits that look like pebbles and can cause infection or a blockage in the gallbladder.

Medications

Less frequently, Gastroparesis is seen to occur after the use of certain medications. Some medications can impair motility. Examples include:

- narcotic pain relievers,
- anticholinergic/antispasmodic agents,
- calcium channel blockers,
- some antidepressants, and
- some medications for diabetes.

Other Illnesses

Aside from these dietary factors, neurologic factors can contribute to GP. Injuries and diseases of the nervous system, such as Parkinson's, can cause GP by damaging the stomach nerves. GP is also commonly seen in persons with multiple sclerosis (MS) and other neurologic disorders. GP can also be caused by illnesses of the connective tissue, such as lupus or scleroderma. The disease process causes weakness in the stomach's smooth muscles, which causes this. Because of these diseases, smooth muscles break down all over the body, including in the GI tract. It is the smooth muscles' job to contract and apply pressure on the body's interior organs and blood arteries.

Cellular Changes

The root causes of Gastroparesis are still poorly understood. It has recently come to light that alterations in the cells that assist in regulating muscle contractions (motility) in the stomach are of particular relevance in idiopathic and diabetic Gastroparesis. Interstitial cells of Cajal, to give them their proper name (ICCs). These cells are essentially the gastrointestinal (GI) system's heartbeat regulators. Scientists are investigating ICCs as a possible contributor to the illness process in Gastroparesis, but they are also considering alterations in the structure and number of nerve cells and immune cells.

CHAPTER 3: OVERVIEW OF GASTROPARESIS SYMPTOMS

Gastroparesis is characterized by a set of chronic symptoms, including:

- The term "abdominal pain" refers to a range of sensations from a dull ache to a strong stabbing sensation that originates from the digestive organs, most commonly the stomach and intestines.
- Nausea is a bad feeling of being sick that can show up in the chest, throat, or head. It can sometimes be accompanied by the urge to throw up.
- Vomiting is the process of bringing food from the stomach into the mouth.
- A painful sensation in the esophagus is caused by acid reflux. It is the esophagus that carries food from the mouth to the stomach.
- Feeling full or satiated quickly after eating a relatively small amount.

Other Symptoms that People Experience

- Some people with Gastroparesis, especially those whose symptoms progress to a more severe state, also report abdominal bloating and pain or discomfort.
- Reduced hunger is a potential factor in weight loss.
- Reflux, or heartburn, can develop when the stomach empties too slowly.

If symptoms of gastroesophageal reflux disease (GERD), such as heartburn or regurgitation, do not respond to treatment, a gastric emptying test to look for delayed stomach emptying may be performed (Gastroparesis).

GP symptoms can sometimes lead to more health problems that make life less enjoyable overall. People who feel sick, have stomach pain or feel full before they should be more likely to be malnourished. Malnutrition occurs when the body fails to absorb sufficient nutrients, particularly vitamins. Any combination of GP symptoms can affect a patient's quality of life by making them sad, making it hard for them to sleep, or making their digestion worse because they can't eat as much.

The symptoms of Gastroparesis might vary greatly between individuals. Symptoms usually appear during and after a meal.

It should be noted that the severity of symptoms in a person with Gastroparesis does not always correlate with how rapidly the stomach empties.

DIAGNOSIS & TESTS

Various tests may be used to diagnose Gastroparesis (GP). This will reveal whether or not something is keeping the stomach from emptying normally. These tests will determine whether the GP symptoms are the result of another ailment.

This may include:

- imaging tests
- blood tests
- upper endoscopy
- An ultrasound, uses sound waves that create images to look for disease in the pancreas or gallbladder that may be causing symptoms.

An endoscopy uses an endoscope, which is a long, flexible tube with a camera and light at the end. During an endoscopy, this tube goes into the mouth, down the esophagus, into the stomach, and into the duodenum. The first part of the small intestine is the duodenum. This tube has a camera and light at the end, which lets the doctor see inside your GI tract and make sure your symptoms are not caused by an ulcer, cancer, or something else.

Your doctor or nurse will decide which tests are best for you. This choice will be made based on how bad your symptoms are, what medicines you take, what's available, and what other health problems you have. The following tests are often used to figure out what's wrong with GP. Drugs that are being taken should also be looked at before a test because some of them can change the results.

If the doctor thinks you have Gastroparesis based on your symptoms, medical history, and physical exam, they will need to do a test to see how fast your stomach empties.

Stomach Emptying Tests

There are different ways to figure out how long it takes for food to move from the stomach to the small intestine. Scintigraphy, a wireless motility capsule, or a breath test are some of these. Your doctor will tell you more about the one that was chosen.

Gastric Emptying Scintigraphy (GES)

A gastric emptying study is the best way to find out if a person has Gastroparesis (scintigraphy). The test is done in a hospital or a center for specialists.

For a gastric emptying scintigraphy, a small amount of a radioactive substance is put in a meal. This lets pictures be taken during digestion, which helps figure out how fast the stomach empties.

Eggs, butter, jam, and toast are often part of the meal. People who are allergic to these foods will get a modified meal that should have the same number of calories and ingredients as the standard meal. The meal should be eaten in its entirety. The test can be done in anywhere from 2 to 4 hours. If the test is done for the full four hours, the results will be the most accurate.

When 10% or more of a meal is still in the stomach after 4 hours, this is a sign of Gastroparesis.

Wireless Motility Capsule

This is a piece of gear that looks like a pill. This pill is taken by mouth and then goes through the digestive system. It will measure the temperature, how the whole gut contracts as the pill move down, and the pH levels (how acidic or alkaline the GI tract is). This information is gathered by wearing a receiver that records data for 5 days. This test also checks how long it takes for the GI tract to move food through the gut.

Gastric Emptying Breath Test (GEBT)

This test is done by taking a sample of your breath. To start the test, the person is given a meal that has an ingredient that is not radioactive. This makes it possible to measure and track the food in your breath over a few hours. This test can be done at home or in a doctor's office to see how fast the stomach empties.

Some people with Gastroparesis have symptoms that are so bad that changing their diet and taking medicine isn't enough to help. People's quality of life can be greatly hurt by symptoms that make them unable to do things. When treatment doesn't work, symptoms that don't go away (refractory) can lead to life-threatening dehydration, loss of essential minerals (electrolyte imbalances), and malnutrition that requires hospitalization. Then, special treatments to help with the problem may be thought about. Some of these are:

- enteral nutrition,
- parenteral nutrition,
- gastric electrical stimulation, or
- other surgical procedures.

ENTERAL NUTRITION

Enteral nutrition is when a feeding tube is used to put liquid food into the digestive tract. It is used when eating by mouth is not enough to get enough nutrition. In more severe cases of Gastroparesis, or endoscopy, a radiology team or surgeons may put a tube in the stomach and small intestine. This tube is called a G/J tube, which stands for Gastrostomy-Jejunostomy tube. By putting the tube in the small intestines, it can help people with Gastroparesis, a condition that makes it hard for the stomach to empty, to avoid the stomach. A 6 to 12-inch tube comes out of the stomach or small intestines. This tube can be used to administer nutritional formulas as well as medications. This is taken care of with the help of a doctor and a dietitian.

PARENTERAL NUTRITION

For people with severe Gastroparesis who can't eat by mouth or through a tube, an intravenous (IV) catheter may be used to give them nutrition without going through the GI tract. This is called a PICC line and is often put in the arm. A small, flexible tube called an IV catheter is put into a vein. The formula that goes into the catheter is made to give the body nutrients that it does not need to break down. This lets the body take in the nutrients directly through the blood.

G-POEM

G-Poem is an abbreviation for gastric perioral endoscopic myotomy, which is a surgery in which the pyloric muscle is cut so that the pyloric muscle can open. This could help some patients better empty their stomachs. This procedure is done by a surgeon or an advanced endoscopist.

GASTRIC ELECTRIC STIMULATION (GES)

A small device that is surgically implanted under the skin in the lower part of the abdomen for a certain group of patients with GP who have not been helped by other GP treatments. GES has been shown to make people vomit less often and feel less sick, but it does not help the stomach empty faster.

Through a Humanitarian Use Device exemption, the FDA has given its OK for Enterra therapy. The device can be put in through a laparoscope, which makes surgery less likely to cause problems. Once the battery-powered device is in place, its settings can be changed to find the best way to control symptoms.

In 2000, the FDA approved the first Enterra device. In 2015, the FDA approved Enterra II, a second-generation device. The newer device gives doctors more ways to use the system and makes it easier to do so.

Enterra therapy is not a cure, so other types of treatment must still be used. If the therapy does not work, the device can be taken out.

OTHER SURGICAL PROCEDURES

When all other treatments fail, some patients may try other surgical procedures.

- Venting the stomach through a gastrostomy (a tube that goes into the stomach) keeps air and fluid from building up in the stomach and may help people who are very sick and keep throwing up.
- Both pyloroplasty and gastrojejunostomy are surgeries that try to help the stomach empty. Pyloroplasty widens the lower part of the stomach, and gastrojejunostomy connects the stomach to the jejunum part of the small intestine.
- Gastrectomy is a surgery in which part or all of the stomach is removed. Researchers are still looking into how well these procedures work to treat Gastroparesis.

These procedures should only be thought of for certain patients with special needs and situations after all other options have been carefully discussed and weighed.

CHAPTER 5: DIETARY & LIFESTYLE MEASURES

Scientists need to find out more about how each person with Gastroparesis should eat to get the best results. At the moment, dietary advice is based on what foods tend to speed up or slow down the emptying of the stomach.

A registered dietitian (RD) or nutrition support specialist (nurse or doctor) can help make a diet plan that fits each person's needs. The dietician will work with the patient to find the right combination of solid, semi-solid, and liquid foods for the person.

Care should be taken to make sure that the right nutritional needs are met. Nutrients are the things in food that your body needs to stay healthy. There are proteins, carbs, fats, vitamins, minerals, and water among them. When treating Gastroparesis, the goal is to change the balance of nutrients, not to get rid of any of them.

People with diabetes will need to keep their blood sugar levels as stable as possible. After the stomach empties into the small intestine, the blood glucose level goes up, but in people with Gastroparesis, this doesn't happen as often as it should.

GENERAL RECOMMENDATIONS

Most people with Gastroparesis do well if they eat small, low-fat meals on a regular basis. Fat, fiber and big meals can slow down how quickly the stomach empties. Eating 4-6 small meals each day will help you stay healthy.

Eggs, peanut butter, and lean meats are all good sources of protein. Choose foods that are easy to chew, and make sure to chew well before swallowing. If you need to, you can turn solid foods into liquids by adding juice or water to a blender. Most people can handle cooked or juiced vegetables well.

Avoid rough fruits and vegetables, foods with seeds, nuts, and skins or husks that can't be eaten. Carbonated drinks can make bloating and distension worse.

By adding nutritional supplements like caloric drinks, protein powders, or protein bars, more help can be given.

Don't drink too much or smoke too much. They can make it take longer for the stomach to empty.

CHAPTER 6: GENERAL DIETARY RECOMMENDATIONS

The tips below will help you make smart decisions about the meals you eat and the ones you should avoid.

Dietary guidelines for people with Gastroparesis often consist of the following:

- Eat more frequently and in smaller portions.
- Cut back on the greasy stuff.
- Don't eat fiber
- The inability to properly chew foods should be avoided.

Some examples of recommended meals are:

- Canned meats, processed cheeses, and ground or pureed meats
- Vegetables, if needed, blended or filtered after cooking

- Fruits that have been cooked and, if necessary, blended/strained
- Fruit drinks, milk products, and other liquids, if tolerated
- Eat frequently, but not too much

When the size of a meal is cut down, the stomach doesn't get as full. If you eat smaller meals, you might not feel as full or bloated, and your stomach might empty more quickly. Since the size of meals is getting smaller, people need to eat four to six times a day to get enough nutrition.

AVOID FOODS HIGH IN FAT

Fat can slow down how quickly the stomach empties. Food will stay in your stomach for less time if it contains less fat. But liquids with fat, like milkshakes, might be OK and give you the calories you need.

A DIET LOW IN FIBER IS SUGGESTED

Fiber slows the emptying of the stomach. Also, fiber can stick together and make it hard for the stomach to move.

Foods high in fiber that you should stay away from include the following:

- Fruits such as apples, berries, coconuts, figs, oranges, and persimmons
- Green beans, green peas, lettuce, potato peels, and sauerkraut are all vegetables.
- Whole grain cereals with bran

Fleshy fruits with little seeds Beans, lentils, and soya beans are all examples of legumes/dried beans. Similarly, if at all possible, people should stop using fiber supplements as a means of treating constipation.

DO NOT EAT ANYTHING THAT MAY BE DIFFICULT TO CHEW.

Examples of hard-to-chew foods include: Broccoli, Corn, Popcorn, Seeds, Nuts

Chew food well before swallowing.

It takes longer for the stomach to empty when there is solid food in it. When teeth are damaged or missing, it can be difficult to chew food properly. This could make it even harder for the stomach to break down food into smaller pieces that can be absorbed in the small intestine.

Position

It has been suggested that drinking fluids while eating and remaining upright for half an hour after eating can aid in digestion and digestion by allowing the stomach to empty.

Vitamins and minerals

If your body is not getting enough nutrients from food alone, try taking a multivitamin and mineral supplement every day.

CHAPTER 7: RECOMMENDATIONS FOR A NUTRITIONAL DIET IN GASTROPARESIS

The stomach takes longer to empty when there is no blockage. This is a sign of Gastroparesis. Oftentimes, doctors don't know what causes Gastroparesis in these patients. Several other illnesses, including diabetes, have been linked to its occurrence. Women are disproportionately affected, and it can have serious consequences for their well-being.

Most of the time, people with Gastroparesis are treated by: Diet changes, medicines that help the empty stomach faster, and medicines that stop nausea and vomiting.

Clinical experience is relied upon heavily when making dietary recommendations for patients with Gastroparesis. In order to establish which foods individuals with Gastroparesis can tolerate better than others, there is a need for additional research in the scientific community.

It is recommended that those who have been diagnosed with Gastroparesis seek dietary counseling with a doctor and a Registered Dietician in order to assist in individualizing their nutrition therapy and make the most of the nutritional benefits.

The people who are most likely to benefit the most from dietary suggestions are those who are already dealing with mild to moderate conditions. In addition, patients with more severe cases of Gastroparesis are given these treatments as an adjunct to other types of medical care.

LIQUIDS

If following the standard dietary recommendations is not sufficient to keep your Gastroparesis under control, you may be given the recommendation to consume the majority of your meals in the form of semi-solids or liquids, such as puréed foods or soups. Patients who have Gastroparesis typically have normal stomach evacuation of drinks despite their condition. Drinks like Hawaiian Punch and Hi-C, which contain calories in addition to hydration, are better than water alone since they deliver both fluid and calories.

Some things you can do while on a liquid diet are: Custard , Cereals (soft/easy to chew), Smoothies, Milk, Instant breakfast, Yogurt, Puddings, Milkshakes

SUPPLEMENTS

You might need to add a liquid nutrient preparation that is low in fiber to your diet to get all the nutrients you need to meet your nutritional needs. Some examples of such preparations include Ensure and Boost, but you might also use baby meals.

As an additional source of liquid nutrients, foods that have been blended can also be employed. Blenders are able to process any food. When working with solid meals, it is necessary to dilute them with a liquid of some kind, such as stock, milk, juice, or water. Always make sure to give the blender a thorough cleaning after using it.

MEDICATIONS TO AVOID

There are quite a few medications that can delay stomach emptying. Tell your doctor about all the medications you are taking and ask if any could be slowing down your stomach emptying.

Here are some examples that can slow your stomach emptying:

- Aluminum-containing antacids (Amphojel)
- Narcotic pain medications (Percocet, Tylenol #3, Oxycontin, and others)
- Anticholinergic agents (Bentyl, Levsin, Elavil, and others)
- Bulk-forming agents (Metamucil, Perdiem, Fibercon, and others)

DIABETES

If you have diabetes as the cause of your Gastroparesis, one of your primary goals should be to attain and then maintain a satisfactory level of glucose control. Monitoring insulin levels and blood sugar levels on a more regular basis makes this process much simpler and more effective. Maintaining a healthy blood sugar level may facilitate the emptying of the stomach. If your blood sugar level is always over 200, you should let your primary care doctor know.

CHAPTER 8: SAMPLE MEAL PLANS

If you have Gastroparesis, eating more frequently but in smaller portions might help you feel less full. In order to keep your nutritional intake at the same level as before, you will need to eat four to six meals every day.

Based on what has been learned about how long it takes for the stomach to empty after eating different kinds of food, a number of dietary suggestions have been made. Individuals with mild to moderate conditions are most likely to benefit from these dietary recommendations; nevertheless, they are frequently explored in patients with more severe Gastroparesis to complement existing medical treatments.

The following are some sample meal plans for consuming six smaller meals over the course of one day. Meal plans tailored to your specific needs can be crafted with the assistance of both your primary care physician and a Registered Dietitian.

TRY THIS SAMPLE MEAL PLAN

Breakfast

- ½ cup grape juice
- 1 scrambled egg
- 1 cup cream of wheat cereal
- ½ cup skim milk

Snack

- 10 ounces of instant breakfast with skim milk

Lunch

- ½ cup applesauce
- ½ cup milk
- 1 tablespoon mayonnaise
- ½ cup vegetable soup
- ½ turkey sandwich

Snack

- 10 ounces banana shake made with l plain or vanilla yogurt, milk, and sugar

Dinner

- 2–3 ounces of baked chicken or fish
- ½ cup mashed potatoes
- ½ cup milk
- ½ cup fruit cocktail
- 1 teaspoon margarine
- ½ cup spinach

SNACK

- ½ cup pudding, custard, or gelatin

TRY A SMOOTHIE INSTEAD

Smoothies are a simple and delectable method that can be used to provide your body with the critical nutrients it needs.

When it comes to what goes into a smoothie and how it can be made to taste different, the options are almost endless. Smoothies can be consumed either as a meal or as a snack.

Banana Pineapple Green Smoothie

- ½ ripe banana
- 1 peeled lemon wedge (1/4 of a lemon)
- 1/2 tablespoon natural peanut butter
- 1/8 teaspoon (or a few dashes) of ground ginger
- 3-4 ice cubes
- ¼ cup frozen pineapple
- 1 cup loosely packed spinach

Instructions:

Combine all ingredients in the blender, and blend 1-2 minutes until smooth

CHAPTER 9: COMPLEMENTARY & ALTERNATIVE MEDICINE

When traditional medical treatments don't work or have unwanted side effects, many people choose to try complementary or alternative medicine (CAM).

Patients can use complementary therapy in addition to traditional forms of medical care. In place of conventional medical care, patients often choose alternative therapies.

The condition known as Gastroparesis has been treated with a few different complementary and alternative medicine (CAM) approaches. Research is required to evaluate the efficacy of complementary and alternative medicine (CAM) treatments for Gastroparesis.

Ginger has been used for centuries in traditional Chinese medicine to relieve nausea. When consumed in amounts that are considered to be safe, ginger has a low risk of causing adverse effects. Gas, bloating, heartburn, and nausea are the side symptoms that people report experiencing most frequently.

Acupuncture has demonstrated, in a number of limited studies, that it may be of assistance in the treatment of Gastroparesis. Fullness and bloating were two of the symptoms that showed improvement in a diabetic gastroparesis patient who participated in a randomized controlled trial that lasted only a few weeks and was treated with a placebo.

Patients must tell all of their healthcare providers about any complementary and alternative medicine (CAM) practices they are using. The things that patients do to take care of their own health should be completely written down so that medical professionals can use them. This will help guarantee that patients receive care that is coordinated and safe.

CHAPTER 10.1: TIPS ON FINDING A DOCTOR

There are specific characteristics that you should seek for in your doctor, whether he or she is a general practitioner or a specialist (such as a gastroenterologist) so that you can receive the treatment that you require your Gastroparesis.

Here is a checklist of questions to consider:

- Is your physician empathetic toward you? When you describe your symptoms, does he or she pay attention to what you say? Does he or she have a true comprehension of the effect that Gastroparesis has on your life? It is time to find a new doctor if you have the impression that your current one regards your symptoms as unimportant or as being "all in your head."
- Does your physician take the necessary amount of time to explain and talk to you about your Gastroparesis?
- Does your doctor request a lot of tests but neglect to explain why they're being done and what the results mean?
- Does your doctor often prescribe medications or diets without telling you what the possible side effects or benefits might be?
- Are you able to get an appointment in a timely manner that suits your needs?
- Is your primary care physician typically accessible, or do you frequently consult with a substitute who is not knowledgeable about your condition?
- Does it seem that your doctor is knowledgeable about your sickness while also being prepared to seek the counsel of a specialist for challenging issues?

Do you feel confident in the doctor's abilities? If so, this is probably the most significant question. Are you able to develop positive relationships with people? Because Gastroparesis is a chronic illness, its course is likely to change in unexpected ways as time passes. You will benefit the most from having a doctor who is on your side during this process.

Although there is no such thing as a perfect doctor, the responses to the questions presented above should assist you in making a decision. Keep in mind that you are not tied down to your physician in any way. You have the legal right to change doctors and to have your whole medical history transferred to the new practice. On the other hand, making an excessive number of adjustments could work against you.

There are many different factors that can influence one's health or disease. Some things you cannot control, but some you can.

If you have Gastroparesis, it is likely that it will motivate you to continually be looking for what helps, does not help, hurts, and works best for you. This is in addition to adopting healthy lifestyle choices. Even if it isn't always simple, figuring this out can help you improve the aspects of your life that are relevant to your health.

When managing Gastroparesis, it is important to keep the following in mind at all times. Preventative measures can help you alleviate symptoms, reduce negative consequences in your daily life, and improve your overall health and wellbeing.

BE AWARE OF CAUSES AND COMPLICATIONS

If you are able to recognize the symptoms of Gastroparesis, as well as the source of the condition and the difficulties that can result from it, you can help minimize unnecessary delays in seeking the required treatment.

Although the cause is unknown in most cases (idiopathic), Gastroparesis can be a complication of diabetes in roughly one-quarter of people who have the condition and have had the disease for a long time.

Gastroparesis can also arise:

- As a problem following certain surgical procedures (particularly esophageal or upper abdominal surgeries) Following the use of particular medications, such as narcotic pain relievers, anticholinergic/antispasmodic agents, calcium channel blockers, certain antidepressants, and certain diabetes medications
- In conjunction with conditions that affect the entire body, the neurological system, or the connective tissue, such as multiple sclerosis, cerebral palsy, Parkinson's disease, systemic lupus, and scleroderma.

Gastroparesis can lead to:

- Severe loss of body water as a result of constant vomiting
- Individuals diagnosed with diabetes and Gastroparesis sometimes have a difficult time controlling their blood glucose levels (also known as blood sugar).
- The creation of clumps of food that has not been digested, known as bezoars, can cause stomach pain, vomiting, or even a blockage.
- Malnutrition that results from insufficient nutritional absorption or inadequate calorie consumption

- Adverse events brought on by interactions between medications (treatments often may involve taking different classes of drugs to treat several symptoms, such as to reduce nausea, reduce pain, and lower blood glucose levels)

PREVENTION AND MANAGEMENT TIPS

- Collaborate with a registered dietitian (RD) or nutrition support professional (nurse or doctor) to develop a diet plan that is tailored to your specific requirements; get knowledgeable about how to implement and maintain dietary and nutritional therapy.
- Consume many little meals throughout the day that are low in fat and high in fiber. The emptying of the stomach can be slowed down and made worse by the presence of fat, fiber, and heavy meals.
- Maintain a healthy level of hydration and try to get as many nutrients as you can.
- If you have diabetes, it's important to keep your blood sugar levels under control. An irregular emptying of the stomach might have a harmful impact on blood sugar levels. Maintaining a healthy blood sugar level may facilitate the emptying of the stomach.
- Ask your doctor, surgeon, or other members of your healthcare team about the potential dangers associated with surgery, and weigh those risks against the potential benefits. Inquire about the available options.
- Notify both your primary care physician and your pharmacist about any prescription and over-the-counter medications, as well as any dietary supplements, that you are currently taking.
- Keep an eye out for any drug interactions, and talk to your physician about other treatment options.
- Gain an understanding of the potential adverse effects that may be caused by your therapies and practice what to do in such cases.
- Avoid or cut back significantly on drinking alcohol and smoking tobacco. These things can impede the emptying of the stomach.
- To the best of your ability, make engaging in regular physical activity a priority.

Seek the necessary medical attention, and play an active role in managing your health. Working with your primary care doctor or other members of your healthcare team will help you deal with, reduce, or stop problems and symptoms.

TIPS FOR VACATION ENJOYMENT

Gastroparesis is a condition in which the stomach empties too slowly, vomiting, pain, causing nausea, bloating, feeling full, and/or reflux. There aren't many good ways to treat the condition, so most people with it change what they eat and how they live to reduce their symptoms.

Taking care of Gastroparesis at home can be hard, but traveling makes it even harder. With the right planning, though, you can spend time away from family and friends without letting your symptoms get worse.

Before You Go

- Make sure that your needs are taken into account when you plan a trip.
- If you're going to stay in a hotel, ask for a room with a small fridge or kitchenette. This gives you the freedom to store some of your own food and/or make some of it.
- If you are staying with friends or family, let them know about your health condition and any food restrictions that come with it. Either give a detailed list of what you can and can't eat, or let them know that you will bring and cook your own food.
- If you're flying and need to bring liquid meal replacements or medicine on board, call the TSA at 866-289-9673 to make special arrangements. If you have an Enterra gastric neurostimulator, pack the device identification card in your carry-on luggage so you can show it at all security checkpoints.
- Keep a running list of foods that are safe for you to eat when you have Gastroparesis. This will be helpful when eating out at a restaurant.
- Pack nutrient-dense, portable snacks for travel days and a lot of staple foods that are good for people with Gastroparesis for the whole trip.
- Pack all of the medicines, supplements, remedies, and tools for dealing with symptoms that you use at home, both regularly and when you need them or in an emergency.
- If smoothies, purees, or protein shakes are a regular part of your diet, buy a portable blender that you can use when you get to your destination.

Travel Day

Bring your own food and pack twice as much as you think you'll need, no matter how you're getting around. There are often delays, and you can never be sure if there will be food options along the way that is good for people with Gastroparesis.

If you have Gastroparesis, you may find that you get car sick more often than you did before. Have different ways to stop feeling sick on your hand, just in case.

As much as possible, stick to your usual meal plan. Eat well-balanced mini-meals at regular intervals instead of snacking all day, which is likely to give you little nutrition and leave you feeling full but unsatisfied.

Don't eat in the car or while walking through the airport. Instead, eat in a calm place. Take a few deep breaths to calm down before you eat, and chew your food well to help it go down.

Once You Arrive

- Keep doing what you've been doing, both in terms of what you eat and how you spend your time. For example, if you usually do yoga or relaxation exercises in the morning, the plan that into your daily schedule.
- Make every bite and sip as healthy as possible. Now is not the time to eat foods that make you feel full but don't give you any nutrients. If you don't eat well, you might not have enough energy to fully enjoy your trip.
- Try things out carefully and on purpose. Don't decide on the spot to try something you wouldn't normally eat at home. Make sure you have the time and freedom to rest if you feel sick afterward.
- Find ways to treat yourself that don't involve food, such as going to the spa or buying a unique souvenir.
- Move around a lot, especially after you eat. A lot of people find that walking helps them feel better and helps their digestion. It's also a great way to get to know the place you're going on vacation.
- Be sure to drink a lot of water, especially if you're flying, going on a warm vacation, or doing a lot of physical activity. Dehydration can make nausea and vomiting worse, as well as give you headaches and make you feel dizzy.
- Respect your limits and let yourself rest if you're tired or have other symptoms.
- Have fun! Taking care of Gastroparesis can be hard, especially when you're on vacation, but if you follow these tips, you'll be able to enjoy your time away more.

QUICK TIPS
Gastroparesis-friendly

foods are low in fat, fiber, nuts, seeds, skins, hulls, peels, and other indigestible portions.

If something meets these criteria, it is not likely to cause problems. But people have very different levels of tolerance. Not all people with Gastroparesis can eat all of the foods that are good for them. In the same way, some people with Gastroparesis can eat foods that aren't technically good for them. To find out what works best for you, you have to try things out carefully.

Gastroparesis-Friendly Foods That Can Be Packed

Orgain (no refrigeration needed; pour over ice when ready to drink) Peanut Butter & Jelly

Almond Butter MacroBars PB2: Peanut Butter in powder form (stir into non-fat or low-fat yogurt for added protein and nutrients)

Instant Cream of Wheat in small packages(use a small banana, sliced or mashed, and a tablespoon of PB2 or creamy peanut butter; prepare with water or skim milk).

Cereals like Rice Krispies, Corn Flakes, and Special K that are low in fiber (add skim, soy, rice, or almond milk)

Crackers with less fiber or graham crackers with less fat (spread with nut butter)

Smooth peanut butter or smooth almond butter in single-serving packs (spread on toast, English muffins, or bagels)

Servings of applesauce, peaches, or pears that come in a can (stir into low-fat cottage cheese, Greek yogurt, or non-dairy yogurt)

Nausea Remedies

Ginger has been used for a long time as a natural way to treat nausea. It may also help the stomach empty faster. The Ginger People's Gin-Gins Boost candies have 30% fresh ginger and are easy to put in your purse or pocket.

Nauzene is an over-the-counter medicine that can help with nausea and stomach acid. It comes in cherry-flavored chewable tablets.

QueaseEASE is an inhaler that smells good and has a mixture of lavender, peppermint, ginger, and spearmint oils that help with nausea. It can be taken with you and doesn't make you sleepy.

CHAPTER 12: EVALUATING DISEASE IMPACT AND MEDICATION RISK

KEY FINDINGS

Over half of those who answered would be willing to cut their life expectancy by 11 years or more if it meant they would be in perfect health.

Impact on health: When asked about their current health, 75% of those who answered said it was 50 or below on a scale where 0 is the worst possible health (or as bad as death) and 100 is a normal, healthy life.

Effects of dug-out: When the FDA takes off-the-market drugs that treat Gastroparesis, 48% of patients are very unhappy.

91% of people want drugs to stay on the market with warnings and precautions so that patients and doctors can make safe decisions based on information.

Respondents were asked how much of a risk they would be willing to take for a drug that completely got rid of all of their gastroparesis symptoms.

27% of those who answered are willing to risk a 1 in 100 chance or higher of serious, disabling, or even fatal side effects.

IMPACT OF GASTROPARESIS ON HEALTH

Respondents rated how their health was affected by Gastroparesis, with 0 being the worst (or as bad as death) and 100 is a normal, healthy life.

- The average
- answer was 42, and 75% of the people who answered said their health was 50 or less.

Respondents thought that a new drug would let them live the rest of their lives in perfect health, even if they had Gastroparesis until they were 100 years old. They were asked how many years of their lives they would be willing to lose if they took this medicine.

- 34% of those who answered would be willing to cut their life expectancy by 11 to 20 years.
- 15% of people would be willing to cut 21 to 30 years off their life expectancy to be healthy.

Almost half of the people who answered would be willing to cut 11 to 30 years off their life expectancy if it meant they would be healthy the whole time.

EVALUATING RISK ASSOCIATED WITH MEDICATIONS

Respondents were asked how much of a risk they would be willing to take in order to get rid of all of their gastroparesis symptoms. There is a chance of death, bad things could happen, or there could be mild side effects.

Risk of Death

From a 1 in 10 million chance of death (very unlikely) to a 1 in 2 chance of death (50 percent chance), the answer choices included "would not take the chance of death."

- 6 people said that they would be willing to take a 50% chance of dying.
- 10% of those who answered are willing to take a chance with a 10% or higher chance of dying.

Only 21 of the 168 people who answered this question in the survey are not willing to take some risk of death.

Risk of Serious Adverse Events

Some of the serious side effects that could happen were severe headaches, dizziness, joint pain, or heart problems that made it hard to do your usual things.

Less than 6% are willing to think about these side effects if they have a 10% or higher chance of happening.

- 21% would take no risk.
- 24% of people would take a chance of 1 in 10 million.

Over 80% of those who respond are willing to take risks that have little to no chance of causing serious Harm.

Risk of Mild Side Effects

Possible mild side effects could include feeling sick, tired, or dizzy, but they wouldn't stop you from doing your usual things.

- Less than 4% of people wouldn't risk having mild side effects.
- More than 38% of those who respond will have a 10% chance or higher of having mild side effects.
- More than half of the patients who were asked are willing to take the risk of 1 in 100 or higher.

REGULATORY INFLUENCE

Patients were asked what they thought about decisions made by the U.S. Food and Drug Administration (FDA) about medicines that could cause side effects or other problems. Respondents were asked to imagine the following scenario: "You've been taking a medicine for more than a year, and it's been helping you feel better. The FDA then decides that the drug could hurt other people, such as by causing heart disease. Some people aren't sure if this is really the case, so the FDA took the drug off the market until the question of Harm could be answered.

Impact of Drug Removal on Patients Without Side Effects

Patients would be impacted by this decision, even if they have not had any side effects.

- 17% feel that they would be completely negatively impacted.
- 23% do not feel this decision would impact them.
- 31% would be impacted a great deal.

77% would be impacted by this decision in some way.

Continuing Medication After Market Removal

Responders showed their level of concern for continuing the rest of their medication supply, considering they have shown no side effects up to that point.

- 63% would have little to no concern about continuing this medication.
- 8% would be completely worried about continuing the medication.

Concern that Removed Medication has Caused Harm.

While keeping in mind the current state of health, symptom relief with medication, and lack of negative side effects, participants were asked if they would believe the medication has already done Harm to their bodies.

- 62% would have little to no concern that Harm has been done.
- 3% would be completely concerned.

Satisfaction of Drug Removal

In an effort to protect the public from a potentially harmful medication, we asked participants to assume the FDA removes this medication until safety can be established.

- 51% would prefer the medication be placed back on the market.
- 13% prefer the medication to remain off the market.

Investigational Drug Precautions

Respondents were asked to think about the following rules about keeping an investigational drug on the market. Each line includes all of the above warnings.

1. There would be a warning label, but there wouldn't be any other rules (black box warning).
2. The doctor and the patient would both sign a form saying they were aware of the possible risks.
3. Only a GI specialist could write a prescription for medicine.
4. Every month, you would have to get a new prescription.
5. The GI specialist will fill out an application for use, and the patient will sign to show that they understand the possible side effects of each prescription.

A black box warning is a strict labeling requirement set by the FDA for medicines that are known to have side effects that could be serious or even life-threatening.

- Because of the precautions and warnings, 9% of people say they would no longer take medicine.

- 29% think that a black box warning would be enough, and 24% think that this warning, plus the doctor and patient signing an agreement that there could be bad side effects, would be enough.
- 38% of people think that this medicine should only be given by a specialist in the digestive system, with possible restrictions in place.

CHAPTER 12: ABOUT THE STUDY

Focused and long-term research on Gastroparesis is a must if we want to learn more about this debilitating disease and find ways to help people who have it. IFFGD has always been at the front of the pack when it comes to encouraging and funding researchers in GI illness. Since 1993, the IFFGD has done research surveys to learn more about people with multiple GI disorders and find out what they need. From a survey about how fecal incontinence affects patients' lives to surveys about IBS and Gastroparesis, the IFFGD is always reaching out to the community to find out more about how illness affects people. Through our research awards, we try to get researchers and clinicians to work together and share their research. We help people with GI illnesses and their families all over the world by helping with research, advocacy, educational websites, patient education, and publications.

Late in 2019, the IFFGD asked people with Gastroparesis to fill out a short survey about their quality of life, how bad their disease was, and how they thought their risk was when it came to medications and clinical trials. The IFFGD sent this survey to people with Gastroparesis through email and social media. "Gastroparesis Disease Impact and Medication Risk Assessment" is the name of this survey. During the five weeks that the survey was open, 200 people filled it out, which gave us important information about what gastroparesis patients need and want.

This survey, which had 18 questions and 3 sections, asked about 1) the effect of Gastroparesis on quality of life, 2) the risk versus benefit of improving quality of life, and 3) people's thoughts on high-risk medications. Eighty-four percent of the people who started this survey also finished it. Here are some highlights of what they said. This document gives important information about what the gastroparesis community wants, needs, and thinks. As we learn more about Gastroparesis through scientific and medical research, it is important that patients are a key part of the process from the beginning to the end.

Every answer in this study came from a person who struggles every day to understand and deal with Gastroparesis. Even though most of them are connected to healthcare providers and getting some kind of treatment, their symptoms are still bothersome, and their disorder has a big effect on their lives. People who took part in this survey were honest about what kind of help they needed and what risks they would be willing to take to get it. We're glad that the people who filled out the survey helped us learn more about what the community needs.

CHAPTER 13: ABOUT GASTROPARESIS

Gastroparesis (GP) is a condition in which the stomach takes longer to empty, but there is no obvious blockage or obstruction. Food may move more slowly through the stomach and small intestine, or it may stop moving at all. People with Gastroparesis may have any or all of the following signs and symptoms;

- Abdominal pain is pain that starts in the stomach or intestines and can be dull or sharp.
- Nausea is when you feel sick and want to throw up.
- When someone throws up, food comes back up from the stomach.
- Early satiety is when you feel full quickly or can't eat a full meal.
- Burning in the esophagus is a sign of reflux.
- Unwanted weight loss is when someone loses weight without trying.

Gastroparesis is classified under three diagnoses;

- Idiopathic: The cause is unknown.
- Diabetes-related nerve damage in diabetics.
- Post-surgical: caused by wounds or scars after surgery.

PART TWO: GASTROPARESIS RECIPES

CHATPER 1: BREAKFAST RECIPES

AVOCADO PANCAKES

Preparation Time 5 mins **Cooking Time** 5 mins **Total Time** 10 mins **Serves** 1–2

Ingredients

- 1 avocado
- 60g self-raising flour
- 175g milk
- 1 egg
- Pinch of Salt
- Lime juice
- Oil or butter for frying
- Serve with goat's cheese and salsa verde

Instructions

1. First, remove the avocado flesh from the pit and mash it with some salt and lime juice.
2. The egg and the avocado should be mixed together, and then the milk should be added and combined.
3. Measure the flour and a little bit of Salt. Mix the wet and dry materials together until everything is evenly distributed.
4. Put some fat in a hot pan, like oil or butter. A small amount of batter can be poured in and left to cook on one side. The pancake is done when you can gently flip it over without tearing it. The food should be served hot.

Top tips for making avocado pancakes

Depending on the toppings you choose, you may want to adjust the recipe accordingly. Poached eggs can be given a spicy kick by mixing in some chopped chili to the batter. To sweeten the bacon batter, stir in 1 tablespoon of maple syrup. If using blueberries, some can be pressed into the batter before cooking.

Nutrition

Calories 320 Kcal   Sugar 5 g Salt 0.25 g Protein 10.5 g Carbohydrates 26.4 g

CREAMY MUSHROOM PANCAKES

Prep Time: 30 mins **Cook Time:** 10 to 30 mins **Servings:** Serves 1

Ingredients

- 1 large free-range egg, lightly beaten
- 160ml/5½fl oz milk
- 40g/1½oz plain flour
- knob of unsalted butter
- 4 spring onions, thinly sliced
- 200g/7oz chestnut mushrooms, sliced
- 2 tbsp reduced-fat crème fraîche
- ½ tsp Dijon mustard
- salt and freshly ground pepper

Instructions

1. In a shallow basin or cup, combine the egg and milk using a whisk.
2. Sprinkle a lot of Salt and pepper on the flour and put it in a big basin. Make a well in the middle and add the egg and milk mixture. Add them to the flour a little at a time and mix until you have a batter. Leave aside.
3. Butter should be heated in a large frying pan over medium heat until foaming but not browned or burning. Cook the spring onions until soft, then stir in the rest of the onion, keeping some of the green parts aside. The mushrooms should be added and cooked until tender. Mix in the mustard and crème fraîche, then season to taste. Place in a bowl, tent with foil, and keep hot.
4. Clear the pan and melt a tiny bit of butter over medium heat. Pour half of the batter into the pan's center and evenly distribute it across the pan's bottom. Flip when the bottom is a light golden color and continue cooking until both sides are a deep golden color. Put one aside and create a second pancake in the same way.
5. Arrange the pancakes on a serving platter, and then divide the mushrooms among them. Create a square by folding the edges in, starting with the bottom. Serve with a sprinkling of the remaining spring onion.

Recipe Tips

- For a heartier meal, pair it with a large salad prepared in a basic vinaigrette.
- Use whichever mushrooms you can find, but chestnut mushrooms are typically more affordable and flavorful than button mushrooms.
- Use regular mustard if you don't have Dijon mustard.

KEY LIME PIE PANCAKES

Prep Time: 15 Minutes **Cook Time:** 25 Minutes **Total Time:** 40 Minutes

Servings: 5 Servings

Ingredients
Graham Crumbles

- 1/4 cup melted salted butter
- 1/2 cup whole wheat or graham flour
- 1/2 cup granulated sugar
- ¼ cup flax seed ground
- 1 white egg
- 1/8 teaspoon of Salt

Pancake Batter

- ¼ cup butter, melted
- 2 eggs
- 1 egg yolk
- 6 fluid ounces buttermilk (3/4 cup)
- 1/2 cup water (4 fluid ounces)
- 5 key lime
- juice, 1/4 cup grated zest from 5 key limes
- 2 teaspoons brown sugar
- a tsp vanilla extract
- 2 cups regular flour
- two tbsp baking powder
- Dash of Salt

Lime Syrup

- Juice from 4 key limes
- 5 fluid ounces of sweetened condensed milk (½ can)

Whipping Cream

- 1 cup whipping cream
- 1 tablespoon maple syrup
- ½ teaspoon vanilla extract

Instructions

For the Graham Crumbles:

- Prepare a 350F oven.
- Softened butter, flour, brown sugar, and crushed flax seed are combined with a pastry blender. When the mixture is evenly crumbly, add the egg white and mix again.
- The mixture should be spread out on a baking sheet. Crumble the dough with your fingers until it resembles streusel.
- Put it in the oven and set the timer for 10 minutes. Turn the mixture over and continue baking for another 10 minutes or until the edges are crisp.

For the Pancakes:

1. In the meantime, heat a griddle to 375 degrees Fahrenheit or a nonstick pan over low heat.
2. Beat the egg and egg yolk into the melted butter.
3. Buttermilk, water, lime zest and juice, brown sugar, and vanilla extract are whisked into the mixture.
4. Mix in the flour, baking soda, and Salt using a whisk. Batter needs to sit for 5 minutes before it can be cooked.
5. Pancakes can be cooked by dropping by a spoonful onto a griddle or frying pan that has been preheated. Roast for 3–4 minutes before flipping and roasting for another 2–3 minutes.

For the Lime Syrup:

- Stir together the lime juice and sweetened condensed milk.

For the Whipping Cream:

1. Whip the heavy cream, maple syrup, and vanilla using the whisk attachment of a hand mixer until stiff peaks form.
2. To serve, stack the pancakes with lime syrup, whipped cream, and streusel crumbs.

Notes

- This recipe yields roughly 15 pancakes.
- The condiments are included in the calorie count.
- Key limes can be replaced with regular limes.

Nutrition Information

Serving: 3pancakes, **Calories:** 868kcal, **Carbohydrates**: 99g, **Protein:** 16g, **Sugar:** 47g

GINGERBREAD MUFFINS WITH SWEET LEMON GLAZE

Prep Time: 15 Minutes **Cook Time:** 20 Minutes **Total Time:** 50 Minutes

Yield: 12-14

Ingredients
Gingerbread Muffins

- 1/2 cup (1 stick or 115g) unsalted butter
- 3/4 cup (234g) dark molasses*
- 2 and 2/3 cups (334g) all-purpose flour
- 1 and 1/2 teaspoons baking soda
- 1/4 teaspoon salt
- 1 and 1/2 teaspoons of ground cinnamon
- 1 and 1/4 teaspoons of ground ginger
- 1/2 teaspoon ground cloves
- 1/2 cup (100g) packed light or dark brown sugar
- 1 large egg at room temperature
- 1/2 cup (120g) plain yogurt or sour cream at room temperature
- 1/2 cup (120ml) milk at room temperature*
- optional: coarse sugar for sprinkling

Lemon Glaze

- 1 cup (120g) confectioners' sugar
- 2 Tablespoons fresh lemon juice
- 1 Tablespoon (15ml) milk

Instructions

1. Turn the oven temperature up to 425 degrees Fahrenheit (218 degrees Celsius). Spread some butter or nonstick spray on a muffin tin, or use paper liners. Leave aside.
2. Reduce the size of the butter cubes, so they melt more quickly. Heat the butter and molasses together in a large microwave-safe bowl for 1 minute on high power. Mix it all together with a whisk. Put aside to chill while you combine the dry ingredients.
3. In a large bowl, combine the flour, baking soda, Salt, cinnamon, ginger, and cloves.
4. Whisk the brown sugar, egg, yogurt, and milk into the molasses/butter mixture until everything is incorporated. Add the liquids to the dry and mix *just* until everything is incorporated. Avoid over-blending. It's normal for the batter to be on the thick and lumpy side.

5. Fill each well in the prepared muffin tin to the top with the batter. Coarse sugar can be sprinkled on top for extra crunch if desired. Muffins need to be baked at 425 degrees Fahrenheit for 5 minutes, then at 350 degrees Fahrenheit (177 degrees Celsius) for another 15 to 16 minutes until the tops are cracked, and the centers are set. Check it out with a toothpick. The recommended cooling time in the pan is 5-10 minutes before glazing and serving.

6. While the muffins are cooling, make the glaze by combining all of the ingredients for the lemon glaze in a medium bowl. To adjust the consistency, more powdered sugar can be used, or milk can be added. Add a drizzle to freshly baked muffins. As the icing hardens as the muffins cool, they are convenient for storage and transit.

7. Muffins, whether frosted or unfrosted, can be stored in an airtight container for up to two days at room temperature or seven days in the fridge. Either plain or frosted muffins can be frozen for up to three months. Let it defrost in the fridge or on the counter.

LEMON MUFFINS

Prep Time 10 Minutes **Cook Time** 17 Minutes **Total Time** 27 Minutes

Yield 12

Ingredients
For the muffins:

- 1 3/4 cups (250g) all-purpose flour
- 1 1/2 teaspoons baking powder
- 1/2 teaspoon baking soda
- 1/4 teaspoon salt
- 2/3 cup (135g) granulated sugar
- 2 large eggs
- 3/4 cup yogurt
- 6 tablespoons (85g) butter, melted
- zest and juice of one lemon
- 1/2 teaspoon vanilla extract (optional)

For the lemon drizzle topping:

- 1 cup powdered sugar
- 2-3 tablespoons lemon juice

Instructions

To make the muffins:

1. Set oven temperature to 220C/425F. Prepare a muffin tin with butter or liner sheets for 12 muffins.
2. Sift flour, baking powder, baking soda, and Salt into a large basin; add sugar and lemon zest and stir to combine.
3. Eggs, yogurt, melted butter, lemon juice, and vanilla extract are whisked together in a medium bowl until just incorporated. The wet ingredients are poured into the dry and mixed together using a wooden spoon or rubber spatula. The mixture should not be over-stirred. A thick, lumpy batter is ideal. Fill the muffin tins to the same level with the batter. After 3 minutes, turn the heat down to 180°C/350°F and bake for another 12-17 minutes, or until a toothpick inserted in the center of a muffin comes out clean. After ten minutes, transfer to a wire rack to cool fully.

To make the lemon drizzle topping:

1. Sift the powdered sugar that is contained in the low-volume bowl. Add lemon juice until you obtain desired consistency.
2. After the muffins have had time to cool, drizzle the glaze over the top of them.
3. Muffins taste the best when they are consumed on the same day that they are made; however, they can be kept in the refrigerator for up to three days in an airtight container, or they can be frozen for up to two months.

BANANA PANCAKES

Total Time: 20 Minutes

Ingredients

For Pancakes

- ½ cup all-purpose flour leveled off
- 2 tbsp sugar
- 2½ teaspoon baking powder
- ½ teaspoon of Salt
- 1 peeled tiny overripe banana
- two large eggs
- 1 cup plus 2 tbsp low-fat milk
- ½ tsp vanilla extract

- 3 tablespoons melted unsalted butter

For Cooking

- 1 to 2 tbsp vegetable oil
- 1 tbsp. unsalted butter

For Serving

- Maple syrup
- Sliced bananas
- Confectioners' sugar (optional)

Instructions

1. All-purpose flour, sugar, baking powder, and Salt should be combined in a medium basin and whisked together.
2. Smash the banana with a fork in a bowl until it's almost completely smooth. Blend the eggs with the milk and vanilla extract by whisking them together. Combine the melted butter and banana mixture by pouring it into the flour. Don't overmix the batter; gently fold it together with a rubber spatula until everything is incorporated. You can expect a thick, lumpy batter.
3. Heat a griddle or a pan that won't stick over medium heat. Swirl the griddle with a pad of butter and 1 tablespoon of vegetable oil. Spread the batter out on the griddle by dropping 1/4 cupful at a time. About 2 minutes of cooking time should be enough for the underside to get golden and a few holes to appear on top of each pancake. After 1 to 2 minutes, flip the pancakes over and continue cooking until both sides are golden brown and the pancakes have puffed. You can use the spatula to move the pancakes from the skillet to a serving platter.
4. You should use paper towels to wipe the griddle before re-greasing it with butter and oil and cooking the remaining batter. While the pancakes are still warm, serve them with maple syrup, sliced bananas, and powdered sugar.
5. Freezer-Friendly Instructions: Pancakes are suitable for long-term storage in the freezer (up to three months). Put a sheet of parchment or wax paper in between each pancake and stack them when they're cool. Whether you're using aluminum foil or a sturdy freezer bag, be sure to seal the pancake stack tightly. Put them in a single layer on a baking sheet and cover them with foil to reheat. Put in a preheated oven and bake for 8 to 10 minutes, or until hot.

Nutrition Information

Per serving: Serving size: 2 pancakes Calories:278 Carbohydrates: 35 g Sugar: 9 g Fiber: 1 g Protein: 7 g

VANILLA MANGO MUFFINS

Prep Time 15 Mins **Cook Time** 15 Mins **Total Time** 30 Mins

Servings: 12

Equipment

- mixing bowl
- Whisk
- Mini blender or immersion blender
- 12-hole muffin pan
- Oven

Ingredients

- 1 ripe mango or 1 cup/250g mango puree
- 1¾ cups (225g) all purpose flour (plain flour)
- ¾ cup granulated white sugar
- 2 teaspoons baking powder
- ¼ teaspoon salt
- 2 eggs
- ½ cup (125g) butter melted and cooled slightly
- 2 teaspoons vanilla extract

Instructions

1. Prepare a muffin tin with paper liners and preheat the oven to 400 degrees Fahrenheit (200 degrees Celsius).
2. After separating the flesh of the mango from the pit and the skin, the flesh can be puréed using an immersion hand blender.
3. In a large mixing basin, combine and whisk together the flour, sugar, baking powder, and Salt.
4. Take one cup of the mango puree, measure it out, and put it in a jug with the eggs. The rest of the mango puree can be used for anything else. After giving it a good whisking, add the butter that has been melted along with the vanilla extract to the dry ingredients.
5. To blend, beat for approximately one minute.
6. Put three-quarters of the batter into each well of the muffin tin, then place it in the oven for about 15 minutes, or until the muffins have risen and a toothpick inserted in one of them comes out clean.

7. After allowing to cool in the pan for five minutes, transfer to a wire rack to finish cooling for the remaining time.

Notes

- It is important not to overfill the muffin liners, since this could cause the batter to leak out. Fill them up to about two thirds of the way. For the best results and most uniformly sized muffins, use a scoop designed for ice cream.
- Allow the muffins to cool completely before serving them. This will allow the muffins to come to room temperature, which will help them hold together more securely.
- Before adding the melted butter to the mixture, make sure it has had some time to cool off somewhat so that the eggs are not cooked by the butter.
- Make sure not to overwork the batter. When all-purpose flour is overmixed, it has the potential to make the batter tough, which does not result in a muffin with a pleasant texture.

Variations

- Some vegan chocolate chips, dark chocolate chips, or white chocolate chunks would be delicious mixed in for some added sweetness.
- You can make mango berry muffins by simply adding some fresh berries to the batter.
- Add a tropical twist to the muffin mix by folding in some sweetened coconut.
- Mix in some chopped nuts like walnuts, pecans, or cashews, and sprinkle some on top before baking for more flavor and texture.

Nutrition

Calories: 206kcal | Carbohydrates: 29g | Protein: 3g | Polyunsaturated Fat: 1g | Potassium: 129mg | Fiber: 1g | Sugar: 15g |

DOUBLE CHOCOLATE CHIP MUFFINS

Prep Time: 10 Minutes **Cook Time**: 21 Minutes **Total Time**: 40 Minutes

Yield: 12-14 Muffins

Ingredients

- 2 cups (250g) all-purpose flour
- 1 cup (200g) granulated sugar
- 1/2 cup (41g) unsweetened natural cocoa powder
- 1 teaspoon baking soda
- 1/2 teaspoon salt

- 1 and 3/4 cups (315g) semi-sweet chocolate chips
- 2 large eggs, at room temperature
- 3/4 cup (185g) full fat sour cream or plain yogurt, at room temperature
- 1/2 cup (120ml) vegetable oil*
- 1/2 cup (120ml) whole milk, at room temperature
- 1 and 1/2 teaspoons pure vanilla extract

Instructions

1. Turn the oven temperature up to 425 degrees Fahrenheit (218 degrees Celsius). Prepare a 12-cup muffin tin with nonstick cooking spray or paper liners. About 14 muffins can be made from this recipe, so have a second muffin tin ready in the same way, or bake in two batches, keeping the remaining mixture at room temperature.
2. In a large bowl, mix the flour, sugar, cocoa powder, baking soda, Salt, and chocolate chips. Leave aside.
3. Beat together the egg whites, sour cream, oil, milk, and vanilla extract. Pour liquids into dry and mix thoroughly with a wooden spoon or rubber spatula. (Because the batter is rather thick, a whisk isn't the best tool for the job.) Don't over-stir. We can expect a sticky, thick batter.
4. Put the batter in the liners until they are almost full. Keep the muffins in the oven for another 5 minutes at 425°F, and then lower the heat to 350°F (177C). Continue cooking for 15 to 16 minutes more, or until a toothpick inserted in the center comes out clean. The baking time for these muffins is roughly 20-21 minutes. (Mini muffins need 13–14 minutes in the oven at 350 °F (177 °C) for the full baking time.)
5. Wait 10 minutes before removing the muffins from the pan to cool completely.
6. You can keep leftover muffins in an airtight container at room temperature for up to 5 days, or in the fridge for up to a week.

Notes

- Freezing The muffins can be stored in the freezer for up to three months. Keep in the fridge overnight to defrost, then reheat in the microwave.
- If you'd prefer to make a smaller batch of giant muffins rather than 12 regular-sized ones, simply follow the recipe through step 3 using a greased jumbo 6-count muffin tin. Scoop the batter into the paper cups until they are almost full. Keep the muffins in the oven for another 5 minutes at 425°F, and then lower the heat to 350°F (177C). Add 25–28 more minutes of baking time, or until a toothpick inserted in the center comes out clean.
- To get the full sour cream flavor, use full-fat sour cream. Plain yogurt can stand in for it in a pinch.

- Oil: Use vegetable oil for the greatest flavor and texture. You can use olive oil or canola oil as a substitute if you're out of the original. If you want to attempt making muffins using melted coconut oil, you need to make sure all of the other ingredients are at room temperature so the oil doesn't solidify while you're mixing the batter.
- The best milk to drink is whole milk. Any kind of milk will do; 2%, 1%, or even nondairy will do in a hurry. Never use low-fat or nonfat milk. Avoid buttermilk whenever possible. (You could substitute buttermilk for the sour cream and the milk, but the muffins would have a different texture and flavor as a result.

APRICOT MUFFIN RECIPE

Prep Time: 15 Minutes **Cook Time**: 20 Minutes **Total Time**: 35 Minutes

Servings: 12

Ingredients

- 2 cups all-purpose flour
- 1 egg
- 3/4 cup granulated sugar
- 1 cup Greek yogurt
- 1/2 cup melted butter
- 1 teaspoon baking soda
- 1/2 teaspoon salt
- 2 Tablespoons milk or oil
- 1 cup chopped dried apricots

Instructions

1. Have your oven ready at 350 degrees Fahrenheit. Line muffin tins with cupcake liners.
2. Put two cups of water in the microwave and heat it until it boils. To soften the apricots, soak them in boiling water for five minutes. Leave aside.
3. Combine all of the dry ingredients in a large bowl. Dig a hole in the middle and put it aside. In a separate bowl, whisk together the melted butter, egg, and milk with the yogurt. Add the liquid to the dry and stir until incorporated. Try not to over-blend.
4. Add the drained apricots to the mixture. Smoothly fold it in.
5. Two-thirds of the way up the paper liners with cupcake batter is excellent (an ice cream scoop works perfectly for this). For 20 to 24 minutes, or until the tops are golden and a toothpick inserted in the center comes out clean, bake the muffins.

MUSHROOM OMELETTE RECIPE

Prep Time: 10 Minutes **Cook Time:** 20 Minutes **Total Time:** 30 Minutes

Servings: 3 People **Calories:** 398kcal

Ingredients
For The Filling

- 2 tablespoons extra virgin olive oil
- 1 teaspoon chopped garlic
- 1 cup chopped onions
- 200 grams sliced mushrooms
- 1 teaspoon dried parsley
- ½ teaspoon salt
- ½ teaspoon black pepper powder
- 1 cup shredded cheddar cheese divided
- 1 cup chopped spinach divided

For The Eggs

- 6 large eggs
- 3 teaspoon milk divided
- ¾ teaspoon salt divided

Instructions
Cook The Mushrooms

1. Olive oil should be heated in a large skillet set over medium heat.
2. Fry the garlic for 20 to 30 seconds once the oil is hot.
3. Fry the onions in a little bit of oil until they turn pink, turning often.
4. Cook for another 5-6 minutes after adding the mushrooms. Make sure to stir the food often while it's cooking.
5. Mix in the parsley, Salt, and black pepper.
6. Keep cooking and stirring often until the mushrooms are dry.
7. Turn off the stove and put away the pan.

Whisk The Eggs

1. While the mushrooms are in the oven, crack two eggs into a small basin and whisk them with a fork or wire whisk.
2. Blend in 1 tsp of milk and 1/4 tsp of Salt.

Make The Omelette

1. Pan, nonstick, 6 inches in diameter; heat over low to medium heat.
2. Oil the pan very little.
3. Add the beaten eggs to the skillet.
4. Put a lid on the pan and leave the eggs alone to cook for about nine minutes.
5. Take the cover off and save a couple of tablespoons of the mushroom mixture for the other eggs. The spinach should be diced and some cheese should be kept on top.
6. To serve, crease the omelet in half.
7. Place on a hot serving dish and enjoy.
8. Complete the remaining omelettes in the same fashion.

Notes

- You can use any type of mushroom you like for this dish; however, button mushrooms are what I usually use because they are readily accessible and inexpensive.
- Different types of cheese, such as gruyere, fontina, mozzarella, or gouda, can be used in place of cheddar. Amul processed cheese can also be used.
- You can also use crumbled goat cheese or feta cheese in this dish.
- Any combination of cheeses would be delicious in this dish.
- Fry the mushrooms in a wide fan. This will prevent them from steaming each other and instead allow them to fry.
- Add extra veggies like zucchini, broccoli, sweet corn kernels, bell peppers, etc., to the mix, in addition to the mushrooms, to make it even heartier and healthier.

Nutrition

Calories: 398kcal | Carbohydrates: 9g | Protein: 23g | Fiber: 2g | Sugar: 4g

---

FRESH CORN OMELET

Total Time: 25 Minutes **Yield:** 4 Servings.

Ingredients

- 10 large eggs
- 2 tablespoons water
- 1/4 teaspoon salt
- 1/4 teaspoon pepper
- 2 teaspoons plus 2 tablespoons butter, divided
- 1 cup fresh or frozen corn, thawed
- 1/2 cup shredded cheddar cheese

- Fresh salsa

Instructions

1. Mix the eggs, water, Salt, and pepper in a small bowl. Over medium heat, melt 2 teaspoons of butter in a large, nonstick skillet. Stir in corn and simmer for another minute or two until it's fork-tender. Take out of cooking utensil.
2. Melt 1 tablespoon of butter in the same pan over medium heat. Add in half of the beaten eggs. The edges of the mixture should begin to harden almost instantly. As the eggs begin to set, press the cooked parts toward the center and the uncooked eggs will flow below. When the eggs are set, ladle half of the corn onto one side and top with a quarter of the shredded cheese. The omelet should be folded in half. Separate in half and slide onto separate plates.
3. To use up the rest of the filling, butter, and eggs, simply repeat the process. Add salsa if desired.

TOMATO & BASIL OMELETTE

Cooks In 25 minutes

Ingredients

- 2 sprigs of fresh basil
- 3 cherry tomatoes
- 2 large eggs
- olive oil

Instructions

1. Basil leaves should be plucked and torn coarsely.
2. Use a cutting board to split the cherry tomatoes in half.
3. Prepare a bowl for mixing by cracking the eggs into it.
4. Sprinkle a little bit of Salt and pepper over the dish.
5. Use a fork to thoroughly mix everything together.
6. Warm up a small, nonstick pan over low heat. Meanwhile...
7. Turn the heat to high and add the half tablespoon of olive oil to the pan.
8. Add the tomatoes cautiously and cook for 1 minute.
9. Put the basil leaves on top and turn the heat down to low.
10. Gently add the eggs, and then tilt the pan so that they spread out evenly.
11. Toss the eggs in the pan a bit with a fork.

12. When the top of the omelette has set but the bottom is still runny, fold it in half with a spatula; when the underside is golden brown, take the pan off the heat and put the omelette onto a dish.

Nutrition per serving

Calories 230 Sugars 1.4g Salt 0.92g Protein 14.6g Carbs 1.4g Fibre 0.4g

---

TUNA SALAD SANDWICH

Prep Time 10 Mins **Total Time** 10 Mins **Servings** 2 Servings

Yield 1 To 2 Sandwiches

Ingredients

- 1 (5- or 6-ounce) can tuna packed in olive oil, undrained
- 1/3 cup cottage cheese
- 2 tablespoons mayonnaise
- 1/4 cup finely chopped red onion
- 1 celery stalk, finely chopped
- 1 tablespoon capers
- 1 tablespoon lemon juice
- A pinch or two fresh dill, chopped
- 2 tablespoons fresh parsley, minced
- 1 teaspoon Dijon mustard
- 2 slices bread, lightly toasted
- Lettuce, optional
- Sliced tomatoes, optional

Instructions

1. Mix the following materials together: To make the tuna salad, place the tuna, cottage cheese, mayonnaise, red onion, celery, capers, lemon juice, dill, parsley, and Dijon mustard in a medium bowl and mix thoroughly until everything is incorporated.
2. Construct the sandwich by: You can serve tuna salad on toast either open faced or sandwiched between two slices of bread. If you like, you can also add lettuce and tomatoes. Serve on sliced lettuce for an option that is lower in carbs.

SCRAMBLED EGGS WITH VEGETABLES

Total Time: 10 Min. **Makes** 2 Servings

Ingredients

- 4 large eggs, lightly beaten
- 1/4 cup fat-free milk
- 1/2 cup chopped green pepper
- 1/4 cup sliced green onions
- 1/4 teaspoon salt
- 1/8 teaspoon pepper
- 1 small tomato, chopped and seeded

Instructions

1. Eggs and milk should be mixed together in a separate basin. Add green pepper, onions, Salt and pepper. Pour onto a pan that has been lightly oiled. Cook while stirring for about two to three minutes over medium heat, or until the eggs are almost completely set. After adding the tomato, continue cooking while stirring for a thorough setting of the eggs.

FRENCH TOAST

Prep Time 5 mins **Cook Time** 15 mins **Total Time** 20 mins **Servings** 4 servings

Ingredients

- 4 large eggs
- 2/3 cup milk
- 2 tablespoons ground cinnamon
- 8 slices thick bread from the previous day
- Butter
- Maple syrup

Optional

- 1/4 cup triple sec 2 tablespoons freshly grated orange zest
- Fresh berries

Instructions

1. Make the egg mixture: Eggs, milk, and cinnamon should be mixed together in a medium basin using a whisk. Mix in the orange zest and/or triple sec if you're using any of those ingredients. After thoroughly combining the ingredients by whisking them together, transfer the mixture to a shallow bowl that is large enough to accommodate a slice of the bread that will be used.
2. Soak the bread slices in the egg mixture: Put each slice of bread into the milk egg mixture, allowing some of it to soak in.
3. Fry the French toast: Melt some butter in a big skillet over medium high heat. After removing any extra egg mixture from the bread slices with a shake, lay the bread slices on the hot skillet. Fry the French toast on one side until it is browned, then flip it over and fry the other side until it is golden.
4. Serve: Serve the French toast hot with butter, maple syrup, and/or fresh berries.

HEALTHY PORRIDGE BOWL

Prep:10 Mins **Cook:**5 Mins **Serves** 2

Ingredients

- 100g frozen raspberries
- 1 orange, halved, sliced in half, and juiced in half
- Oatmeal with porridge, 150 grams
- 100ml milk
- ½ banana, cut
- 2 tablespoons of almond butter, smooth
- 1 tbsp goji berries
- Chia seeds, one tablespoon

Instructions

1. Place one-half of the raspberries and the entire amount of orange juice in a skillet. Simmer for around five minutes, or until the raspberries have become more pliable.
2. In the meantime, combine the oats, milk, and 450 milliliters of water in a saucepan and whisk until creamy over a low heat. On top, layer the remaining raspberries, the raspberry compote, orange slices, bananas, almond butter, goji berries, and chia seeds.

SPINACH FRITTATA

Prep Time 15 Mins **Cook Time** 25 Mins **Total Time** 40 Mins

Servings 4 Servings

Ingredients

- 9 big eggs
- 2 teaspoons milk
- 1/3 cup (about 1 ounce, 30g) Parmesan cheese, grated
- a quarter teaspoon of Salt
- 1/8 teaspoon black pepper, freshly ground
- 2 tbsp extra-virgin olive oil
- 1 medium sliced onion
- 1 large garlic clove, minced
- optional 2 tablespoons chopped sun-dried tomatoes
- 8 ounces (225g) fresh chopped spinach or more
- two ounces (56g) the goat cheese

Instructions

1. Whisk together the eggs, Parm, milk, Salt, and pepper: Beat the eggs with the milk and Parmesan in a large bowl. Put some salt and pepper in and mix it in. Put aside for a moment.
2. Saute the onions, then the garlic: On medium heat, warm the olive oil in a nonstick, oven-safe pan. Cook the onion for about 4 or 5 minutes, or until it becomes translucent. Then, after a minute longer of cooking time, add the garlic and sun-dried tomatoes.
3. Add the spinach: A handful of spinach at a time, please. Toss the onion around with the tongs. Fresh spinach should be added in batches as it wilts and makes room in the pan.
4. Add the egg mixture: Spread the mixture evenly over the bottom of the pan once the spinach has wilted. Toss the spinach and onion with the egg mixture.
5. To allow the egg mixture to flow below, lift the spinach mixture down the sides of the pan with a spatula.
6. Sprinkle with goat cheese: Scatter goat cheese bits over the top of the frittata mixture.
7. Lower the heat, cover, and cook: Cover the pan and reduce the heat to low. Keep cooking for another 10–13 minutes, or until the edges are firm but the middle is still a

bit loose. (You might have to peek in a few times to verify if the frittata is setting properly.) It's important that the core maintains some give. Turn on the broiler.

8. Finish under the broiler: The best place for the oven rack is the upper tier. Toast the top for 3–4 minutes in the broiler. Using oven mitts, take out the oven and let cool for a while.

FRITTATA WITH TURNIPS AND OLIVES

Time 1 Hour 15 Minutes **Yield:** 6 Servings.

Ingredients

- 1 pound medium or tiny firm turnips
- Salt
- 2 tbsp extra virgin olive oil
- 2 tablespoons minced fresh thyme leaves
- 6 eggs
- 1 teaspoon milk
- ½ cup chopped flat-leaf parsley, freshly ground
- 1 ounce pitted and chopped imported black olives, approximately ⅓ cup
- 1 or 2 minced or puréed garlic cloves

Instructions

1. In a food processor or with a box grater with big holes, shred the peeled turnips. Use a lot of Salt and let it sit in a colander for half an hour. Squeeze the turnips tightly to remove extra water.

2. In a large skillet or saucepan, heat 1 tablespoon of olive oil over low heat. Add the turnips and thyme, and cook until the turnips are tender, about 5 minutes. After the turnips have come to a boil, reduce the heat to low, cover, and simmer for 15 minutes, stirring occasionally. Whenever they start to brown or stick to the pan, a tablespoon of water is the perfect solution. Just add Salt and pepper to taste. Take it off the heat for a moment so it can cool down.

3. Salt and pepper to taste, then beat the eggs and milk together in a bowl. Mix in the chopped olives, garlic, and parsley. Combine the turnips into the mixture.

4. In a large, preferably nonstick, ten-inch skillet, heat the remaining olive oil over medium heat. Place your palm over it; it ought to be warm. You can tell if your pan is ready by dropping in a small amount of egg and listening for the sizzle; if it cooks immediately, the pan is hot enough to use. The eggs should be poured in. To ensure that the eggs and filling are uniformly distributed, swirl the pan. As the frittata begins

to set, give it a quick shake while tilting the pan slightly and raising up the frittata's borders with a spatula to allow the eggs to run below. After the initial few layers of the eggs are cooked, reduce the heat to low, cover, and cook for 10 minutes while gently shaking the pan. To prevent the frittata from burning on the bottom, you should lift the lid and gently loosen the bottom with a spatula while gently tilting the pan.

5. In the meantime, preheat the broiler. Remove the lid and broil for 1 to 3 minutes, keeping a close eye on the dish to ensure the top doesn't burn. Turn off the heat, give the pan a quick shake to loosen the frittata, and set it aside to cool for at least 5 minutes. Use a spatula to loosen up the perimeter. Carefully remove from the pan onto a large round dish. Create bite-sized diamonds by slicing into wedges. You can serve it hot, cold, or at room temperature.

SUMMER SQUASH FRITTATA WITH HERBS

Ingredients

- 2 medium shredded zucchini or other summer squash
- 2 tbsp olive oil
- 1 finely sliced tiny yellow onion
- 2 cloves
- garlic, thinly sliced
- Kosher Salt, freshly ground pepper
- 1 tbsp. unsalted butter
- 12 big eggs, lightly beaten
- ⅓ cup sour cream or crème fraîche
- ¼ cup ricotta cheese
- 2 tbsp Parmesan cheese, finely grated
- 1½ cups fresh tender herbs
- 1 tablespoon fresh lemon juice 2 teaspoons finely grated lemon zest
- Red pepper flakes, crushed

Instructions

1. Get the oven ready at 350 degrees. Do your best to prevent a soggy frittata by squeezing the zucchini with your hands as you work in batches.
2. Prepare a cast-iron pan of 8 or 10 inches in diameter and 1 tablespoon of oil over medium heat. Season the onion and garlic with Salt and pepper and add them to the pan. Cook for 5-8 minutes, stirring periodically, until the onion is softened and beginning to brown. Stir in zucchini and season with Salt and pepper. Stirring

occasionally, cook for 5-8 minutes, or until zucchini is tender and starts to brown. Turn the heat down to low and add the butter, stirring it in until it melts.

3. In a large bowl, beat together the eggs and crème fraîche until fluffy; then, season with Salt and pepper and pour over the veggies. For about 5 minutes, until the edges are just set, cook while whisking the egg mixture and rotating the pan constantly. Sprinkle with Parmesan and dollop with ricotta. Place skillet in oven and bake for 12-15 minutes, or until eggs are slightly puffy and set in the middle. Hold off on serving frittata for at least 10 minutes while the pan cools.

4. In the meantime, whisk together the remaining 1 tablespoon of oil with the herbs, lemon zest, and lemon juice. Add Salt and pepper to taste and place herb salad on top of fritatta. Slice into wedges and sprinkle with red pepper flakes, if desired.

HAM AND CHEESE FRITTATA

Prep Time 10 minutes **Cook Time** 25 minutes **Total Time** 35 minutes **Servings** 8 servings **Calories** 196kcal

Ingredients

- 8 eggs 1 pound Gruyère cheese
- 2 tablespoons heavy whipping cream
- 2 tablespoons unsweetened butter
- 1/4 teaspoon
- salt, 1/4 teaspoon pepper
- 1 shallot (sliced thin)
- 1 lb. smoked ham (or leftover ham, diced)
- parsley, chives, or green onion

Instructions

1. Set oven temperature to 350 degrees Fahrenheit.
2. In a medium bowl, combine the eggs, heavy whipping cream, Salt, and pepper. The Gruyere cheese should be added and stirred in. Putting aside.
3. Butter should be melted in a large Dutch oven or deep oven-safe pan over medium heat. When the oil is hot, add the shallots and fry, stirring regularly, for about 10 minutes, or until the shallots have softened and turned a light brown and caramelized color. Distribute the shallots uniformly on the base of the skillet.
4. Sprinkle the shallots with the egg mixture and carefully pour the egg mixture on top. Add another minute or two of cooking time, or until the frittata begins to firm around

the perimeter. In order to let some of the raw egg slide underneath the frittata, lift up the edge of the pan.

5. Top the frittata with the diced ham. Throw the frittata back in the oven for another 12-15 minutes, or until the middle is still somewhat wiggly. Once it starts cooling, it will set up more.

6. You should cut it into 8 pieces once it has cooled down. Use fresh herbs like parsley, chives, or green onion as a garnish.

Notes

- To prevent the extra starch found in pre-shredded bagged cheese, shred your own from a block.
- This recipe is easily adaptable to fit your preferences. Substitute cheddar or Swiss cheese for the Gruyere. Broccoli, peppers, and/or mushrooms can be added before cooking, and the shallot can be swapped out for onion if you prefer.
- Put the leftovers in a sealed container and place it in the fridge. In a maximum of 4 days, use.

Nutrition

Carbohydrates: 2g | Protein: 14g | Cholesterol: 205mg | Sodium: 451mg | Potassium: 156mg | Fiber: 1g | Sugar: 1g

CARAMELIZED ONION FRITTATA

Serves: 8 **Prep Time:** 10 min **Cook Time:** 20 min

Calories: 228

Ingredients

- 8 large eggs
- 1/3 cup heavy cream
- 1 tsp sea salt
- 1/2 tsp freshly ground black pepper
- 1/4 cup chopped fresh chives
- 6 oz feta, crumbled, divided
- 2 Tbsp extra-virgin olive oil
- 1 cup caramelized onions
- 4 cups baby kale (5oz)

Instructions

1. Get the oven ready by preheating it to 400 degrees Fahrenheit and positioning a rack in the middle. The eggs should be beaten in a big bowl. Blend in the cream, seasonings, and two-thirds of the feta cheese.
2. The olive oil should be heated in an oven-safe 10-inch skillet over medium heat until it shimmers. Cook the kale for 2 minutes in the oil, or until it has wilted. Break up the caramelized onions and add them to the kale, mixing everything together. While the pan is still on medium heat, carefully pour in the egg mixture and leave it alone for 2 minutes to solidify around the edges.
3. Put the pan on the middle oven rack and bake for 10 minutes, or until the eggs are set all the way through but still somewhat soft in the middle.
4. Cut into 8 serving-sized wedges and serve.

ALMOND COATED FRIED CHICKEN

Prep Time: 10 min **Cook Time:** 20 min

Serves: 2

Ingredients

- 1 pinch Black Pepper
- 2 - Chicken Fillets sliced in half lengthways
- 1 - Eggs
- 2 tbsp Milk or almond milk
- 1 tsp Paprika
- 1 pinch Salt
- 80 g SuperValu Ground Almonds

For Frying

- 1 drop Coconut Oil or rapeseed oil

To Serve

- 0.5 - Cucumber for green salad
- 1 handfull Spinach for green salad
- 1 handfull SuperValu Iceberg Lettuce for green salad
- 4 tbsp Sweet Chilli Sauce for dipping

Instructions

1. Whisk the egg and milk together in a shallow bowl. Combine the ground almonds, paprika and seasoning in a second shallow bowl.
2. Dip a chicken strip into the egg mixture, shaking off any excess, then transfer to the ground almonds and coat generously. Set aside and repeat for the remaining strips.
3. Heat a little coconut oil in a frying pan set over a high heat. Add the chicken strips and fry for 2 to 3 minutes on each side, then turn the heat down to medium and continue to cook for about 10 minutes, turning regularly, until the chicken is cooked through.
4. Serve with a green salad and a small bowl of sweet chilli sauce on the side for dipping.

FILET MIGNON STEAK PIZZAIOLA

Prep Time 20 Minutes **Cook Time** 30 Minutes **Total Time** 40 Minutes

Servings 2 **Calories** 580kcal

Ingredients
Filet Mignon Steaks

- Two Prime Ribeye Steaks (6 oz each) (170 g)
- 1/4 cup water 1 tablespoon olive oil, divided
- Salt and pepper

Peppers and Mushrooms:

- 1 tablespoon olive oil
- 1/2 red bell pepper, sliced (2 oz/ 56 g)
- 1/2 green bell pepper, sliced (2 oz/ 56 g)
- 1/4 cup thinly sliced onion (1 oz/ 28 g)
- 4 oz Mushroom slices (113 g)
- 2 tablespoons dry white wine
- 1 tablespoon fresh thyme leaves
- Garlic 2 oz. Parmesan Butter
- Softened unsalted butter (56 g)
- 2 oz Parmesan cheese, grated
- 1/4 teaspoon raw garlic, grated
- Rao's Arrabiatta Sauce, 1/2 cup

Instructions

1. Wait 30 minutes and then handle the steaks. If they try to lay flat, gird them with some baking twine. While that's happening, chop the vegetables and whip up some

Garlic Parmesan Butter. Set oven temperature to 375 degrees Fahrenheit and arrange oven rack in the center of the oven.

2. **Garlic Parmesan Butter:** Combine the grated Parmesan cheese, grated garlic, and melted butter in a mixing bowl. Place a heaping spoonful on a sheet of cling wrap and use the wrap to form the mixture into a log. Keep chilled till use.

3. **Filet Mignon:** Set a skillet that can go from stovetop to oven at medium-high heat. Apply some of the olive oil to your hands and rub the filet mignons all over. Make sure to season all of the meat with Salt and pepper. Salt is a great complement to protein.

4. Add the remaining olive oil and immediately tilt the pan to spread it once the pan is heated. Steaks should be seared for 1 1/2 to 2 minutes.

5. Inject the thermometer into one steak, flip it, and repeat with the other. To cook, put the dish in the oven and set the timer. Take the steaks out of the pan and tent them with foil to keep warm while they rest.

6. **Peppers and Mushrooms:** After preheating the pan, return it to the fire and set the heat to medium. Add the olive oil, onions, and peppers. Keep the vegetables from scorching by sauteing them for about two minutes. We can now incorporate the wine and mushrooms. Add the fresh thyme and cook for a further two to three minutes. Convey to a serving platter immediately.

7. **Sauce:** Remove the skillet from the heat and stir in the red sauce to rewarm it and absorb any lingering flavors.

8. **Plating:** Arrange the sauce in a circular pattern on two plates. Steaks should be centered in the sauce. Spread 1 tablespoon of Parmesan butter atop each. Evenly distribute the vegetables between the two plates. Serving Size: 7.2 g Net Carbs

ZUCCHINI NOODLES RECIPE

Prep: 10 minutes **Cook:** 15 minutes **Total:** 25 minutes

Ingredients

- 20 ounces Zucchini
- 2 tablespoons unsalted butter
- a pinch of sea salt
- The spice black pepper

Instructions

1. **How to Make Zucchini Noodles:** Use a spiralizer to make zucchini noodles.
2. **How to cook zucchini noodles in the oven:** The oven needs to be heated to 375 degrees F. (177 degrees C). Prepare a humongous baking sheet by greasing it.

3. Spread the zucchini out in a single layer on a baking sheet, leaving some space between them. Then, lightly season with sea salt and mix.
4. To achieve an al dente texture, bake for 15 minutes. Use two paper towels to thoroughly dry the zoodles.
5. Blend in melted butter, then season with black pepper and additional Salt if desired.
6. **How to cook zucchini noodles on the stove:** The zucchini noodles should be washed in a colander set over the sink. Add some salt, and stir it all together. Set aside 30 minutes to drain. After a half hour, drain the zoodles by gently squeezing them over the sink. It's not necessary to squeeze out every last drop; only the main part should do.
7. Soften the butter in a large skillet over medium heat. Stir in zucchini and cook for three to four minutes, or until the vegetable is just tender but still firm. Add extra sea salt and black pepper to taste.

SAUTÉED GREEN BEANS WITH CHERRY TOMATOES

Prep Time: 5 minutes **Cook Time:** 15 minutes **Total Time:** 20 minutes

Yield: 4 servings

Ingredients

- 1 1/2 lbs fresh green beans, trimmed and cut into 2 inch pieces
- 1/4 cup butter
- 1 tablespoon sugar
- 1/2 teaspoon garlic powder
- 1/4 teaspoon salt
- 1/4 teaspoon pepper
- 10 oz cherry tomatoes, cut in half
- 1 tablespoon chopped fresh basil

Instructions

1. Green beans should be soaked in water and placed in a big saucepan. Put on the stovetop and bring to a boil over medium heat. Once boiling, turn the heat down to low, cover the pan, and simmer the green beans for about 10 minutes, or until soft. Remove the liquid and set it aside.
2. Over medium heat, melt the butter in a large skillet. The sugar, garlic powder, Salt, and pepper should be mixed in. Once the onions are translucent, add the tomatoes and simmer them down until they are soft, stirring regularly. Add the green beans and

stir them into the tomato sauce. Heat for another minute or two, until the beans are hot. Put the basil in a bowl and serve right away.

Nutrition

Serving Size: 1/4 of recipe Calories: 164 Sugar: 7 g Carbohydrates: 14 g Fiber: 5 g Protein: 4 g Cholesterol: 30 mg

ROASTED CAULIFLOWER RICE

Prep Time 10 minutes **Cook Time** 30 minutes **Total Time** 40 minutes

Yield 4

Ingredients

- 1 medium head cauliflower, see note
- 2 tablespoons olive oil
- 1 teaspoon garlic powder
- 1 teaspoon onion powder
- 1 teaspoon salt
- ½ teaspoon cracked pepper
- fresh herbs, for garnish

Instructions

1. Set oven temperature to 425 degrees.
2. Cauliflower rice, oil, and seasonings should be combined on a broad, rimmed baking sheet. Move the cauliflower around so that it gets coated in the oil and seasonings.
3. In a baking dish, spread the rice out in a uniform layer and bake for 25–30 minutes, stirring once every 10 minutes, or until the cauliflower has reached the desired level of browning. When serving, garnish with chopped fresh herbs.

Notes

- In the produce area of some supermarkets, you can find fresh cauliflower rice. Using this in the dish will be a success. You'll want about 20 ounces, which is about 2 1/2 cups, but the oil and seasoning may be easily adjusted to suit the amount of cauliflower you're using.

CAPRESE SALAD

Prep: 10 min **Total:** 10 min **Yield:** 4 to 6 servings

Ingredients

- 3 vine-ripe tomatoes, 1/4-inch thick slices
- 1 pound fresh mozzarella, 1/4-inch thick slices
- 20 to 30 leaves (about 1 bunch) fresh basil
- Extra-virgin olive oil, for drizzling
- Coarse Salt and pepper

Instructions

1. Arrange tomato and mozzarella slices in alternating layers on a large, shallow tray, punctuating each layer with a basil leaf. Season the salad with Salt and pepper to taste and drizzle it with extra-virgin olive oil.

BUTTERNUT SQUASH SALAD

Prep Time: 20 mins **Cook Time:** 30 mins **Total Time:** 50 mins

Serves 4 as a side

Ingredients

- 1 small peeled, seeded, and cubed
- butternut squash ½ to 1 teaspoon extra-virgin olive oil
- ¼ teaspoon cumin
- ¼ teaspoon coriander
- ¼ teaspoon cinnamon
- ¼ teaspoon cayenne pepper, less if you are sensitive to heat
- 6 cups spring mix greens, loosely packed
- 2 oz. goat cheese, ripped into tiny pieces
- 2 pitted and diced
- Medjool dates
- pomegranate seeds ¼ cup
- ¼ cup crumbled and toasted
- pistachios, sea salt, freshly ground black pepper

Cider Date Dressing (makes extra)

- 5 tbsp extra virgin olive oil
- 2 tbsp. apple cider vinegar
- 1 tablespoon freshly squeezed lemon juice
- ½ garlic cloves 1 Medjool date
- ⅛ teaspoon cumin, sea salt, and black pepper, to taste
- 3–5 tablespoons water, as needed for mixing

Instructions

1. Prepare a large baking sheet by heating the oven to 425 degrees and lining it with parchment paper. Spread the cubed butternut squash on the baking sheet and season with olive oil, Salt, and pepper. Spread out in a single layer on a baking sheet and toss to coat. Roast for 30–35 minutes, turning once, or until tender and browned.
2. Mix the cumin, coriander, cinnamon, and cayenne in a small basin. Putting aside.
3. Method for Preparing Cider Date Dressing: Olive oil, lemon juice,cumin, date, garlic, vinegar, Salt, pepper, and 3 tablespoons of water should all be blended together in a blender. Blending may require an additional 1–2 teaspoons of water.
4. After baking the butternut squash, take it out and toss it in the spice mixture while it is still warm.
5. Spring mix greens and half of the roasted squash should be used to make the salad. Drizzle a third of the dressing over the squash mixture and toss gently. Add the remaining goat cheese, dates, pomegranates, and pistachios and toss again. Add additional dressing if you like. Quickly dish it up.

THE BEST LEFTOVER TURKEY SALAD

Prep Time 10 mins **Cook Time** 0 mins **Total Time** 10 mins

Servings 6 servings

Ingredients

- 4 cups chopped leftover turkey
- 1/2 cup mayonnaise
- 2 teaspoons Dijon mustard
- 1 Tablespoon lemon juice
- 2 teaspoons sugar
- 1/2 cup finely diced celery
- 1/4 cup sliced scallions

- 2 teaspoons chopped fresh dill

Instructions

- Blend together the ground turkey, mayonnaise, mustard, lemon juice, sugar, celery, scallions, and dill in a large bowl.
- To season the turkey salad, taste it and add Salt and pepper to taste. Serve right away or store in the fridge, covered, until needed.

SHRIMP SALAD

Prep Time: 5 mins **Total Time:** 20 mins **Yields:** 2 serving

Ingredients
For salad

- 1 lb. shrimp, peeled and deveined
- 1 tbsp. extra-virgin olive oil
- Kosher Salt
- Freshly ground black pepper
- 1/4 red onion, finely chopped
- 1 stalk celery, finely chopped
- 2 tbsp. freshly chopped dill
- Toasted bread or butterhead or romaine lettuce, for serving

For dressing

- 1/2 c. mayonnaise
- Juice and zest of 1 lemon
- 1 tsp. Dijon mustard

Instructions

1. Firstly, set oven temperature to 400 degrees Fahrenheit. Throw the shrimp on a large baking sheet and drizzle with oil. Season with Salt and pepper.
2. The second step is to bake the shrimp for 5 to 7 minutes, or until they are opaque all the way through.
3. Step 3Mix together mayonnaise, lemon juice and zest, dijon mustard, and Salt and pepper in a large basin using a whisk. Put the shrimp in a basin and toss in the dill, red onion, celery, and dill until everything is evenly distributed. 4Arrived atServe on toast or lettuce.

SALMON EGG SALAD

Ready In:10mins

Ingredients

- 14 -15 ounces canned salmon, flaked
- 6 hard-boiled eggs, peeled and chopped
- 1/2 cup chopped onion
- 1/2 cucumber, peeled, seeded and chopped
- 1 1/2 teaspoons Dijon mustard
- 1/2 - 3/4 cup mayonnaise
- 1/8 teaspoon black pepper
- 1/2 - 3/4 teaspoon dried tarragon
- 1/4 teaspoon paprika
- salt, if needed, to taste

Instructions

1. Combine everything in a bowl and stir until uniform.
2. A few hours in the fridge will let the flavors meld together perfectly.

EASY QUINOA SALAD

Prep Time 10 mins Total Time 10 mins Course: Salad Servings: 6

Calories: 225kcal

Ingredients
For the Dressing:

- 1/4 cup olive oil
- 1 minced garlic clove
- 2 tbsp of lemon juice 1 lemon, big
- 1 tablespoon balsamic vinegar
- 1 tsp pure maple syrup
- To taste, kosher Salt and black pepper

For the Salad:

- 2 cups cooked quinoa, chilled
- 2 cups chopped fresh spinach leaves

- 1 cup cucumber, chopped
- 1 cup grape or cherry tomatoes, halved
- 1 big pitted, peeled, and chopped
- avocado
- 2 sliced green onions
- To taste, kosher Salt and black pepper

Instructions

1. In the beginning, prepare the dressing. Combine the olive oil, garlic, lemon juice, vinegar, maple syrup or honey, Salt, and pepper in a small bowl or jar and whisk to combine. Putting aside.
2. Put the quinoa, spinach, cucumber, tomato, avocado, and green onions in a big bowl and mix everything together.
3. After dressing the salad, drizzle it over the salad and mix gently to combine. Prepare to taste with Salt and pepper. Serve.

Nutrition

Serving: 6g | Calories: 225kcal | Carbohydrates: 19g | Protein: 4g | Fat: 15g |Sugar: 3g | Calcium: 33mg | Iron: 1.7mg

GREEK SALAD

Prep Time: 15 mins **Total Time:** 15 mins **Serves** 4

Ingredients
Dressing

- ¼ cup virgin olive oil
- 3 tablespoons vinegar
- 1 minced garlic clove
- 1/2 teaspoon dried oregano, plus more for sprinkling
- ¼ tsp Dijon mustard
- ¼ tsp sea salt
- ground black pepper, freshly ground

For the salad

- 1 English cucumber, cut lengthwise, seeded, and ¼ -inch thick sliced
- 1 green bell pepper, cut into 1-inch cubes
- 2 cups cherry tomatoes, halved

- ⅓ cup thinly sliced red onion 5 ounces feta cheese, cut into ½ inch cubes*
- ⅓ cup Kalamata olives, pitted
- ⅓ cup mint leaves, fresh

Instructions

1. Prepare the topping: Olive oil, vinegar, garlic, oregano, mustard, Salt, and several twists of pepper should be mixed together in a small bowl.
2. Arrange the cucumber, green pepper, cherry tomatoes, feta cheese, red onions, and olives on a wide serving plate. Pour the dressing over the salad and toss very gently. To finish, sprinkle on some oregano and mint leaves. Taste and adjust seasoning.

AVOCADO SALAD

Prep Time: 10 mins **Total Time:** 10 mins

Ingredients

- 2 avocados - peeled, pitted and diced
- 1 sweet onion, chopped
- 1 green bell pepper, chopped
- 1 large ripe tomato, chopped
- ¼ cup chopped fresh cilantro
- ½ lime, juiced
- salt and pepper to taste

Instructions

In a big bowl, mix together the avocados, onions, peppers, tomatoes, cilantro, and lime juice. Don't overwork it, but stir gently so everything is covered. To taste, add Salt and pepper.

EASY HOMEMADE PIZZA DOUGH

Prep Time: 10 mins **Cook Time:** 15 mins **Additional Time:** 20 mins

Total Time: 45 mins

Ingredients

- 1 cup warm water (110 degrees Fahrenheit/45 degrees Celsius)
- 1 package (.25 ounce) active dry yeast
- 1 tsp. white sugar
- 2 ½ cups bread flour
- 2 tbsp of olive oil
- 1 teaspoon sea salt

Instructions

1. Put in a 450-degree oven (230 degrees C). Oil a pizza pan lightly.
2. Put the yeast and sugar in a bowl with the heated water. It takes around 10 minutes of mixing and standing for the mixture to become creamy.
3. Beat the yeast mixture, flour, oil, and salt until smooth. Do it by hand, or use a stand mixer with a dough hook to speed up the process. Wait 5 minutes before proceeding.
4. Pat or roll the dough out into a 12-inch circle on a lightly floured board. Bring the pizza pan that has been greased.
5. Pizza sauce and your favorite toppings can be spread on the crust.
6. Toast in a hot oven for 15–20 minutes or until the bread is crisp and golden. Take it out of the oven, and let it cool for about 5 minutes, then serve.

Cook's Note:

The crust made with bread flour is better than that made with all-purpose flour.

If you don't want to use grease on your pizza pan, you can use a pizza stone instead.

ZUCCHINI PIZZA BITES

Total: 20 min **Active**: 10 min **Yield**: 12 bites

Ingredients

- Cooking spray
- 1 medium zucchini
- Kosher salt
- 1/4 cup marinara sauce
- 1/2 cup shredded mozzarella

Instructions

1. Put the oven temperature at 400 degrees F. Put some cooking spray on a sheet pan and line it with aluminum foil.
2. You may get about 24 slices by slicing the zucchini 1/4 inch thick. Sprinkle the slices with salt and place them on the baking sheet. Spread half a teaspoon of sauce and a tablespoon of mozzarella on each piece.
3. Bake for about 8 minutes or until the cheese is melted and bubbling.

CAULIFLOWER CHEESE

Prep:10 mins **Cook:**35 mins **Serves** 6

Ingredients

- 1 large cauliflower, broken into pieces
- 500ml milk
- 4 tbsp flour
- 50g butter
- 100g strong cheddar, grated
- 2-3 tbsp breadcrumbs, if you have them

Instructions

1. To cook one large cauliflower, break it up and add it to boiling water in a large pot. Cook for 5 minutes. Take out a piece of cauliflower to see if it's done, and if not, cook for another 5 minutes.
2. After it has been drained, transfer the cauliflower to an oven-safe dish. Preheat the oven to 220° Celsius (200° Fahrenheit) or gas 7.
3. Reheat the saucepan and stir in the remaining ingredients: 500 mL milk, 4 tbsp flour, and 50 g butter.

4. The flour will vanish, and the sauce will thicken if you keep whisking quickly while the butter melts and the mixture comes to a boil. While the sauce bubbles and thickens, whisk it for two minutes.
5. Remove from the heat and pour over the cauliflower, along with the majority of the 100 g of grated cheddar cheese. Sprinkle the remaining cheese and, if using, the breadcrumbs over the top. Bake for 20 minutes or until bubbling.

BEST BROCCOLI OF YOUR LIFE

Prep Time 10 minutes **Cook Time** 25 minutes **Total Time** 35 minutes

Servings 6 **Calories** 129

Ingredients

- 4 lbs broccoli
- 4 garlic cloves, peeled and cut. Before beginning, read the notes section.
- Good olive oil or butter-flavored coconut oil for Keto.
- ½ tablespoons kosher salt
- ½ teaspoon black pepper
- , freshly ground
- 2 tablespoons freshly squeezed lemon juice 2 teaspoons grated lemon zest
- ⅓ cup freshly grated Parmesan

Instructions

1. Turn the oven temperature up to 400 degrees Fahrenheit (200 degrees C).
2. Broccoli florets can be removed from their thick stalks by cutting them off at the base. Leave about an inch or two of stalk attached to each floret and throw away the rest. Separate the florets by cutting the larger parts through the base of the head with a tiny knife. You need roughly 8 cups of florets.
3. Arrange the broccoli florets in a single layer on a baking sheet large enough to do so. Five tablespoons of olive oil, including the minced garlic, should be tossed with the broccoli. Add salt and pepper to taste.
4. Cook in the oven for 20 to 25 minutes or until soft and browned at the tips of the florets.
5. While still hot, combine the broccoli with 1 1/2 teaspoons of olive oil, lemon zest, lemon juice, and Parmesan. In a hot dish.

Notes

The garlic in this dish comes out really crunchy. Unfortunately, some ovens can cause food to burn or turn bitter. Cooked garlic that is too dark for your taste can be avoided by adding it in the last 5–7 minutes of cooking time after it has been lightly coated in oil and spread over the pan.

Don't scrimp on the oil; season thoroughly, and make sure your oven is hot before adding the broccoli.

Broccoli should be washed thoroughly before eating, so: remember to pat dry your broccoli once you've washed it. The crisper it gets, the dryer it needs to be.

If you want your extra broccoli crispy, flip it over halfway through the roasting process. Even though it takes a long time, it turns out perfectly crisp on every side.

Nutrition

Calories: 129 | Carbohydrates: 21g | Protein: 10g | Fiber: 7g | Sugar: 5g |

HAM, CHEESE, AND TOMATO PIZZA

Ready In: 30mins

Ingredients

- 1 pizza crust
- 2 tablespoons pizza sauce
- 1/2 cup ham, chopped
- 1 tablespoon onion, chopped
- 6 cherry tomatoes, quartered
- 1 tablespoon basil
- 1/4 cup parmesan cheese, shredded
- 1/4 cup mozzarella cheese, shredded
- 1/4 cup of tasty cheese, shredded

Instructions

- Cover the crust with the pizza sauce.
- Mix the cheeses together in a basin and sprinkle some of the mixtures over the sauce.
- First, sprinkle the ham and onion over the pizza, followed by the tomato.
- Finish with the remaining basil and cheese.

- Bake for 20 minutes at 180C, or until the base is golden and the cheese is melted and bubbling.

LOW-CALORIE SMOOTHIES

Prep Time 1 minute **Cook Time** 1 minute **Total Time** 2 minutes

Servings 1 smoothie

Ingredients

Smoothie with strawberries

- 1 cup thawed frozen strawberries
- 1/2 cup almond milk, unsweetened

Blueberry smoothie

- 1 cup blueberries, frozen
- 1/2 cup almond milk, unsweetened

Banana smoothie

- 1 frozen banana, large
- 1/2 cup almond milk, unsweetened
- a half teaspoon cinnamon

Smoothie with chocolate

- 1 cup almond milk, unsweetened
- 1 cup of ice
- 1 tablespoon sugar-free hot chocolate mix
- Smoothie with Coffee
- 1 frozen banana, large
- 2 tbsp espresso or brewed coffee
- 1/2 cup of ice
- 1/2 cup almond milk, unsweetened
- Smoothie with greens
- 1 frozen banana, large
- 1/2 cup fresh baby spinach
- 1/2 cup almond milk, unsweetened

Instructions

1. Put the frozen fruit, milk, and whatever else you want in a high-powered blender and blend at high speed until smooth.
2. Get a big glass and start drinking right away.

Nutrition

Calories: 87kcal | Carbohydrates: 10g | Protein: 3g | Fat: 2g | Sodium: 24mg | Potassium: 17mg | Fiber: 5g

HONEY-ROASTED CHERRY & RICOTTA TOAST

Prep Time: 20 mins **Cook Time:** 25 mins **Total Time:** 45 mins

Ingredients

- 12 slices of an Italian baguette, each about 1/4-inch thick
- 26 large, very ripe cherries
- 2 tablespoons honey, plus more for drizzling
- 1–1/2 cups (12 ounces) fresh whole-milk ricotta cheese
- balsamic vinegar for drizzling
- sea salt for sprinkling

Instructions

Set oven temperature to 450 degrees Fahrenheit. Spray a large-rimmed baking sheet with nonstick cooking spray and line it with foil.

Take the time to take the cherry stems off. Too much juice will be lost if the pits are taken out. Spread the cherries out in a uniform layer on the prepared baking sheet and toss them with 2 tablespoons of honey. Allow to roast in the oven for around 15 minutes or until the cherries begin to wrinkle and release their juices.

In the meantime, spread the bread slices out in a single layer on a baking sheet. You can make ricotta as creamy as you want by whipping it in a large bowl with a whisk or in a stand mixer with a whisk attachment.

Put the bread pieces in the oven and toast them for 4 minutes per side, or until golden, after you take the cherry out of the oven.

While the bread is toasting, remove the pits from the cherries by making a shallow cut in the side of each cherry with a knife.

Serve by topping each piece of toast with 2 tablespoons of ricotta, 2-3 pitted cherries, a drizzle of honey, a dollop of balsamic, and a sprinkling of sea salt.

All of the toasts can be served at once, or the ingredients can be set out so that guests can make their own.

EASY MANGO SMOOTHIE BOWL

Prep Time: 10 minutes **Total Time**: 10 minutes **Servings:** 2

Ingredients

- 2 large mangoes
- 1 cup coconut milk
- 1 cup almond milk
- 2 teaspoons honey
- 1 frozen banana

Instructions

1. Blend the frozen banana, mango, both milk, and honey until smooth in a blender.
2. Split the smoothie in half and serve it in two bowls. Add whatever toppings you choose.

CONFETTI WRAPS

Ingredients

- 1 pound ham (about 2 or 3 slices of deli-cut ham)
- 1 pound turkey (about 2 or 3 slices of deli-cut turkey)
- 1 lb Swiss cheese (about 2 slices of deli-cut cheese)
- 1 chopped hard-cooked egg
- 4 finely shredded romaine lettuce leaves (about 1 cup)
- 1/4 cup yellow bell pepper, coarsely chopped
- 1/4 cup minced red onion
- 1/4 cup peeled, seeded, and finely chopped cucumber
- 1 tomato, seeds removed, chopped
- 1 small carrot, grated
- 2 tbsp reduced-calorie Thousand Island dressing
- 2 large, colorful sun-dried tomato wraps

Instructions

1. Roll the ham slices up tightly, and then slice them into thin strips. Wrap the turkey and Swiss cheese in a similar fashion. Mix in chopped or shredded vegetables. Almost dry enough to eat without dressing, your mixture should appear like confetti.

2. Transport it in a disposable plastic bowl. Wrap up the filling and serve with the dressing on the side. Wait to put it together until you're ready to eat. Put some' confetti' on a large tortilla wrap and drizzle on some dressing. Take a spin and relish the ride.

3. You can expect to find around 342 calories, 41 grams of carbohydrates, 21 grams of protein, 10 grams of fat, 703 milligrams of sodium, and 4 grams of fiber in one serving.

4. Gout sufferers can eat this dish with confidence because it has a small number of purines. It's recommended that you eat no more than one or two portions of meat, fish, or poultry every day.

CHOCOLATE-OAT BARS

Prep 20 min **Total** 2 hr 15 min **Servings** 16

Ingredients

- 1 pound semisweet chocolate chips
- 1/3 cup sweetened condensed fat-free milk (from a 14-ounce can)
- 1 cup whole wheat Gold Medal flour
- 1/2 cup quick-cooking or old-fashioned oats
- a half teaspoon baking powder
- a half teaspoon baking soda
- 3/4 cup packed brown sugar
- 1/4 teaspoon salt
- Canola or soybean oil, 1/4 cup
- 1 teaspoon vanilla extract
- 1 egg or 1/4 cup of fat-free, cholesterol-free egg product
- 2 tablespoons quick-cooking or old-fashioned oats
- 2 teaspoons softened butter

Instructions

1. To make the chocolate sauce, combine chocolate chips and milk in a 1-quart heavy pot and cook over low heat, stirring regularly, until the chocolate is melted and the

mixture is smooth. Prepare a 350°F oven. Use cooking spray to coat an 8- or 9-inch square pan.

2. In a large basin, combine the flour, 1/2 cup oats, baking powder, baking soda, and salt. In a medium bowl, whisk together the brown sugar, oil, vanilla, and egg product until smooth; stir this mixture into the flour mixture until well combined. Keep the remaining half cup of dough in the small bowl for the topping.

3. Pat the remaining dough in a pan. Coat the dough with the chocolate mixture. The reserved dough should be mixed with 2 tablespoons of oats and the butter with a pastry blender or fork until crumbled. Spoonfuls of the oat mixture should be dropped equally over the chocolate.

4. Brown and set the top in the oven for 20 to 25 minutes. Allow 1.5 hours for cooling time. Bars should be halved horizontally so that there are four sections.

RICE PUDDING

Prep Time 5 mins **Cook Time** 35 mins **Total Time** 40 mins **Servings** 3 to 4

Ingredients

1. 2 1/2 cups whole milk (600ml)
2. 1/3 cup (66g) (66g) short-grain white rice, uncooked
3. a pinch of salt
4. 1 big egg
5. 1/4 cup (50g) (50g) packed with dark brown sugar
6. a tsp vanilla extract
7. a quarter teaspoon of cinnamon
8. 1/3 cup (40g) (40g) raisins

Instructions

1. Cook the rice in the milk: The milk, rice, and salt should be brought to a boil in a medium heavy-bottomed saucepan over high heat. Simmer, partially covered, for 20-25 minutes or until rice is tender. Keep the rice from sticking to the pan bottom by stirring it often.

2. Combined with the hot cooked rice, the egg and sugar will make: Whisk the egg and brown sugar together in a small bowl until combined. Whisking constantly, gradually add a half cup of the heated rice mixture to the egg mixture.

3. Add the egg mixture back to the pan: Reintroduce the egg mixture to the rice and milk in the pot. Once it starts to boil, turn the heat down to low and keep stirring until the mixture gets thick, or 160 degrees Fahrenheit (71 degrees Celsius).

4. Curdling will occur if the mixture boils, so avoid doing it. Turn off the heat and mix in vanilla extract, raisins, and cinnamon. When warm, the pudding will be on the runny side, but it will thicken as it cools. Serve warm or cold.

CLASSIC LEMON MERINGUE PIE

Prep Time: 6 hours **Cook Time:** 1 hour, 10 minutes **Total Time**: 7 hours, 10 minutes

Yield: one 9-inch pie

Ingredients

- Homemade Pie Crust
- 5 big yolks of eggs
- 1 and a third cup (320ml) water
- 1 cup granulated sugar (200g)
- 1/3 cup (38g) (38g) cornstarch
- a quarter teaspoon of salt
- 1/2 cup (120ml) (120ml) freshly squeezed lemon juice
- 1 teaspoon lemon zest
- 2 teaspoons (28g) room temperature unsalted butter
- Meringue
- 5 big room-temperature
- egg whites
- 1 tablespoon cream of tartar
- 1/2 cup (100g) (100g) sugar, granulated
- a quarter teaspoon of salt

Instructions

1. Pie crust: First thing I do when I'm getting ready to create a lemon meringue pie is make sure the pie crust is ready to go. To give the dough enough time to chill in the fridge before rolling it out and blind baking, I always make pie dough the night.
2. Set oven temperature to 375 degrees Fahrenheit (190 degrees Celsius), and put the oven rack in the bottom third of the oven. Blind bake pie crust in a 9-inch pie dish. While the pie crust is blind baking, you can get a head start on the lemon meringue filling. Since tempering the egg yolks is a time-sensitive part of making the filling, you may want to wait until the crust has finished blind baking before getting started.
3. Reduce the temperature of the oven to 350°F (177°C).

4. Make the filling: In a medium dish or liquid measuring cup, beat the egg yolks until they are homogenous. Putting aside. In a medium saucepan set over medium heat, combine the water, granulated sugar, cornstarch, salt, lemon juice, and lemon zest by whisking all of these ingredients together. After about 6 minutes, the liquid will begin to thicken and bubble. Initially, it will be thin and cloudy. When the mixture has thickened, give it a quick whisk and then set the heat to low.

5. Temper the egg yolks: Add the warm lemon mixture to the beaten egg yolks in a slow, steady stream. Slowly pour the egg yolk mixture into the pot while whisking. Boost the temperature back up to medium. Keep cooking until large bubbles form on the surface of the thickened mixture. Turn off the stove and whisk in the butter. The filling should be spread into the warm, under baked crust. Separate out as you whip up the meringue.

6. Make the meringue: The egg whites and cream of tartar should be beaten together for 1 minute on medium speed with a hand mixer or the whisk attachment of a stand mixer and then for another 4 minutes on high speed until soft peaks form. Then, for another 2 minutes, beat on high speed until stiff glossy peaks form, adding sugar and salt halfway through. Meringue should be spread out over the filling. Make sure the meringue reaches the crust and bakes into it. When done this way, the meringue is less likely to leak.

7. For 20-25 minutes, bake the pie on the rack in the oven's bottom third. When the pie is done, take it out of the oven and set it on a wire rack to cool for an hour before putting it in the fridge to chill. Serve after refrigerating for 4 hours and cutting into slices.

8. Cover leftovers and place in the fridge. Due to its delicate nature, lemon meringue pie is best enjoyed on the day it is made. Even with your best efforts, the meringue will eventually dry out and separate. Consume promptly for optimal taste.

PERFECT LEMONADE

Prep Time 10 mins **Total Time** 10 mins **Servings** 6 servings

Ingredients

- 1 cup sugar (can reduce to 3/4 cup)
- 1-cup water (for the simple syrup)
- 1 cup fresh-squeezed lemon juice
- 2–3 cups cold water to dilute

Instructions

1. Make the simple syrup: A small saucepan of sugar and water simmering on low heat. Remove from heat when sugar has been stirred to dissolve fully.
2. Juice the lemons: First, squeeze your lemons while the water for the simple syrup boils. Juice from 4 to 6 lemons, depending on their size, yields around 1 cup.
3. Mix the lemonade: Juice and sugar water/simple syrup should be combined in a serving pitcher. Taste after adding 2–3 cups of cold water. If you like a weaker mixture, just add more water. More fresh lemon juice can be added if you find the lemonade to be too sweet.
4. Chill and serve: Put it in the fridge for 30–40 minutes. Prepare with ice and lemon slices.

MORNING PIE

Ingredients

- 2 cups cottage cheese
- 4 eggs
- $^2/_3$ cup sugar
- 2 tablespoons all-purpose flour
- 2 teaspoons grated orange rind
- 1 tablespoon orange juice
- ¼ teaspoon orange extract
- 1 teaspoon ground cinnamon
- 1 teaspoon nutmeg

Directions

1. Set oven temperature to 350 degrees Fahrenheit. Cottage cheese should be beaten for 1 minute at high speed in an electric mixer in a big bowl. Blend in the remaining elements. Put the mixture into a ceramic pie plate that is 9 inches in diameter and bake for 50 minutes, or until a knife inserted in the center comes out clean. Cover and chill in the fridge overnight. Garnish with a fruit slice and serve cold.

MINI FRUIT TARTS

Prep Time 30 minutes **Cook Time** 20 minutes **Total Time** 1 hour

Yield 24 tarts

Ingredients

For the Tart Shell:

- 1 package 24-count Bake-and-Break sugar cookie squares OR one roll of sugar cookie dough.

For the No-Bake Cheesecake Filling:

- 8 ounces (227g) cream cheese, softened
- ½ cup (100g) granulated sugar
- 1 teaspoon vanilla extract

For the Topping:

- 6 ounces (177ml) limeade concentrate, thawed
- 1 tablespoon (8g) cornstarch
- ¼ cup (50g) sugar
- Fresh fruit, berries, etc.

Instructions

1. Set oven temperature to 350 degrees Fahrenheit. Put nonstick spray in tiny muffins.
2. Fill each well of a muffin tin with a cookie dough square. Wait 12-16 minutes, or until a toothpick inserted in the center comes out clean. Wait until completely cooled to take out of the pan. If you want to remove the cookies without breaking them, run a butter knife around the perimeter of each one. Make a well in the center of each cookie with your finger or the back of a wooden spoon.
3. Prepare the glaze as the cookies bake, giving it time to cool. Combine the concentrate, cornstarch, and sugar in a small skillet or saucepan. Stirring constantly with a whisk, combine the sugar and cornstarch, and cook until the mixture boils and thickens. Get it away from the stove so it can cool down.
4. The filling should be prepared after the sugar cookie cups and glaze have cooled. Cream cheese, sugar, and vanilla extract are mixed until creamy.
5. Put together the tarts by placing about a spoonful of filling in each cookie cup. Sprinkle on some chopped fruit or fresh berries for garnish. Apply the lime glaze and brush it on.

6. Fruit toppings should be consumed within 3 hours. All the parts can be prepared 24 hours in advance and assembled just before serving. Cookie cups should be kept in an airtight container while filling, and icing should be refrigerated. Once put together, these are tastier when consumed on the day they were prepared.

Recipe Nutrition

Serving: 1tart | Calories: 115kcal | Carbohydrates: 16g | Protein: 1g | Sugar: 12g

ICED TEA RECIPE

Prep Time: 5 minutes **Cook Time:** 10 minutes **Total Time:** 15 minutes

Ingredients

- 8 cups water, divided
- 6 bags of black tea
- 1/3 cup sugar, optional; adjust to taste

Instructions

1. First, bring half of the water to a boil in a saucepan. Put the pot on a serving platter and take it off the heat. Brew time for tea bags is 10 minutes.
2. Take out the used tea bags and discard the water. You can make sweet tea by adding sugar or another sweetener while the tea is still boiling and stirring until the sugar or sweetener is dissolved.
3. Pour in the rest of the water and stir the tea. Put it in the fridge and let it chill completely.
4. If preferred, garnish with fresh mint leaves, lemon slices, and ice.

FRENCH DRESSING

Prep: 5 mins **No cook**

Ingredients

- 1 tsp Dijon mustard
- 2 tbsp white wine vinegar
- 6 tbsp extra virgin olive oil
- a pinch of sugar

Instructions

1. Shake the ingredients in a jam jar or whisk them together in a small bowl: Dijon mustard, white wine vinegar, extra virgin olive oil, a pinch of sugar, salt, and pepper.

CRANBERRY RELISH

Prep Time 20 mins **Total Time** 20 mins **Yield** 3 cups

Ingredients

- 2 cups rinsed raw cranberries
- 2 peeled and cored tart green apples, cut into thick slices
- 1 large, whole seedless orange, cut into sections
- 1 to 2 cups granulated sugar

Instructions

2. Prepare your grinder: If you have an old-fashioned grinder, select the medium-sized plate and place it on the edge of a table over a large basin or pan to collect the fruit mixture as it is ground. When using an older model grinder, placing a bowl underneath is a good idea to catch the juice that always drops down the base.
3. Suppose you don't have access to a traditional grinder. In that case, you can use the grinder attachment on a KitchenAid mixer or a food processor. Just remember not to over-pulse the food processor! Or your savor will turn to mush.
4. Chopping very finely by hand is an option, but it takes work, especially with cranberries.
5. Push fruit through grinder: The cranberries, orange segments, and apple slices should be fed into the blender or food processor. Be sure to add the orange peel! Put the fruit through the grinder in alternating batches to ensure that various fruits are mixed together. You can pulse fruit in a food processor in place of a grinder.
6. Add sugar: A dash of sugar, please. Just wait 45 minutes for the sugar to dissolve at room temperature. Keep refrigerated until ready to use.

CHAI SPICED PEAR BAKED OATMEAL

Prep Time: 5 minutes **Cook Time:** 35 minutes **Total Time:** 40 minutes **Yield:** 9 servings

Ingredients

- 2 large eggs
- 2 tablespoon avocado oil
- ¼ cup pure maple syrup
- 1 teaspoon vanilla extract
- 1 ½ cups milk
- 2.25 cups rolled oats
1. 1 teaspoon baking powder
2. 1 teaspoon ground cinnamon
3. ½ teaspoon cardamom
4. ¼ teaspoon ground ginger
5. ¼ teaspoon fine sea salt
6. 1 medium bartlett pear, diced

Instructions

1. Prepare a 1.5-quart casserole dish or 9-by-9-inch baking dish and heat the oven to 375 degrees Fahrenheit.
2. Whisk Soggy Ingredients: beat eggs, oil, maple syrup, vanilla extract, and milk together in a big bowl.
3. Mix in the flour, baking soda, powder, and salt for the dry ingredients.
4. Add the diced pears and mix gently before placing them in the baking dish. Chopped walnuts can be added as a garnish if desired.
5. Bake until the top is brown and the center is set about 35-40 minutes. It can be served right away in bowls or refrigerated for 20 minutes to cut into squares.
6. Top your pear-baked oatmeal with additional toppings and your sweetener of choice, and dig in!

HOMEMADE BREAKFAST BISCUITS

Prep: 10 mins **Cook:** 12 mins **Total:** 22 mins **Servings:** 5 to 7 servings

Yield: 6 biscuits

Ingredients

- 2 cups (240 grams) all-purpose flour, plus additional as needed
- 1 tbsp. baking powder

- 1/2 teaspoon kosher salt
- a third of a cup of cold shortening
- 1 cup milk
- 3/4 cup milk

Instructions

1. Gather the ingredients. Put a rack in the middle of the oven and preheat the oven to 450 degrees Fahrenheit
2. Together in a large bowl, combine the flour, baking powder, and salt
3. Blend in the shortening with a pastry cutter or two knives until the texture resembles coarse crumbs.
4. To add the milk, make a well in the center of the dry ingredients.
5. Fork stir until the dough barely sticks together. It should still have some lumps; this will help your cookies rise into delicious, airy layers when baking.
6. Dust a tidy tabletop with flour. Biscuit dough needs only a few lights kneads to come together.
7. Flatten the dough into a 1/2-inch thick circle. With a biscuit cutter dusted with flour, cut the dough into rounds measuring 2 1/2 inches in diameter. It's important to press down on the cutter in a straight motion. You can get more biscuits out of the scraps of dough if you reroll it.
8. Put the dough pieces on a baking sheet that hasn't been greased, spacing them out equally.
9. In a preheated oven at 400 degrees for 12 minutes, the biscuits should have risen and turned a pale golden color on top. Enjoy while hot!

CINNAMON-TOASTED OATS

Active: 10 Mins **Total:** 30 Mins **Servings:** 2

Ingredients

- 2 teaspoons canola oil or olive oil
- 1 teaspoon unsalted butter
- ½ cup rolled oats
- ¼ teaspoon cinnamon
- ⅛ teaspoon nutmeg
- 1 teaspoon brown sugar

Instructions

1. Melt the butter and oil over medium heat in a small, nonstick skillet. Coat the oats and add them. Season with cinnamon and nutmeg, then heat and stir for another 4 minutes or until the oats have turned a light golden color.
2. Take off the heat and evenly coat with brown sugar. When done, spread out on a dish to cool completely before serving or storing in an airtight container in the fridge for up to 4 days.

Nutrition Facts

Serving Size: 1/4 cup   Per Serving: 140 calories; protein 2.5g; carbohydrates 15.3g; dietary fiber 2.2g; sugars 2g;

BANANA SMOOTHIE

Prep Time 5 mins **Total Time** 5 mins **Servings:** 1 serving **Calories:** 203kcal

Ingredients

- 1 cup frozen sliced banana, around 1 large banana
- ¼ cup Greek yogurt, plain or vanilla
- ¼ cup milk Dairy, almond, oat milk, etc.
- ¼ teaspoon vanilla extract

Instructions

Throw everything into a high-powered blender. Process until silky smooth, adding additional milk if necessary. Quickly dish it up.

Notes

The smoothie can be made thicker and colder with the addition of frozen bananas. If the banana was not frozen, smoothies could be chilled with the addition of ice cubes.

Smoothie with plain Greek yogurt and whole milk used for calculating nutrition facts.

Nutrition

Serving: 8g | Calories: 203kcal | Carbohydrates: 39g | Protein: 9g | Cholesterol: 9mg | Sodium: 46mg

BLUEBERRY DETOX SMOOTHIE

Prep Time: 10 minutes **Total Time:** 10 minutes **Servings:** 1 **Calories:** 326kcal

Ingredients

- 1 cup wild blueberries, frozen
- 1 tablespoon fresh cilantro leaves
- 1 frozen banana, cut into pieces to facilitate blending
- a quarter avocado
- half a cup of orange juice
- 1/4 cup of water

Instructions

In a blender, combine the blueberries, cilantro, banana, avocado, orange juice, and water. Blend until totally smooth. As soon as possible, serve.

Nutrition

Calories: 326kcal | Carbohydrates: 65g | Protein: 4g

KIDNEY NOURISHING SMOOTHIE

Ingredients

- 1/2 large cucumber
- 1 cup fresh/frozen blueberries
- 1 cup coconut water
- 1-2 Tbsp ground flax or chia seeds
- 1 pinch cinnamon
- 1 squeeze of fresh lime juice
- 1 cup ice
- stevia

Instructions

1. Place all of the ingredients in the Vitamix container in the order that they are stated, then close the container.
2. After turning the machine on, start at speed 1 and quickly work your way up to the highest speed.
3. When necessary, while the food is being processed, use the tamper to properly force the ingredients into the blades.
4. Blend for forty-five to sixty seconds or until the consistency you want is obtained.
5. Put a halt to the machine and start serving.

CRANBERRY DETOX SMOOTHIE

Prep Time: 5 min **Total Time**: 5 min

Ingredients

- 1 cup fresh frozen cranberries
- 1 apple, peeled and cored

- 1/2 cup almond milk
- 1/2 cup water
- 1/2 teaspoon ground cinnamon
- 1/2 teaspoon ground turmeric

Instructions

1. Add all the ingredients into a large blender and blend until smooth
2. Garnish with ground cinnamon and cranberries, if desired

PUMPKIN PIE SMOOTHIE

Prep Time 10 minutes **Cook Time** 0 minutes **Total Time** 10 minutes **Servings** 1 serving

Calories 320 kcal

Ingredients

- 1 frozen banana
- ½ cup plain or vanilla yogurt
- 1/2 cup pumpkin puree
- 1/2 cup unsweetened almond milk
- 1 tablespoon almond or pecan butter
- 1 teaspoon vanilla extract
- 1/2 teaspoon ground cinnamon
- pinch each nutmeg, ginger & allspice

Instructions

Put all of the ingredients in a blender and process them until they are completely smooth.

Recipe Notes

If you don't have cinnamon, ginger, and nutmeg, you can use pumpkin pie spice instead.

Use your favorite dairy-free yogurt to make something dairy-free.

BLACKBERRY SMOOTHIE

Prep: 5 mins **Cook:** 0 mins **Total:** 5 mins

Ingredients

- 1 banana sliced and frozen
- 1 cup frozen blackberries
- 1 small diced apple
- 1 cup unsweetened vanilla almond milk or milk of your choice
- 1/2 cup vanilla yogurt
- 2 dried dates pitted
- 1 tablespoon ground flaxseed meal
- 2 teaspoons ground cinnamon
- 1/2 teaspoon pure vanilla extract

Instructions

1. Collect, cut, and measure out the constituents of the smoothie.
2. A banana, some blackberries, and an apple should be blended with some milk. Yogurt, dates, flaxseed, cinnamon, and vanilla extract.
3. Get a smooth consistency by pureeing. Quickly dish it up.

Nutrition

Serving: 1of 2 Calories: 235kcal Carbohydrates: 48g Protein: 6g Fiber: 10g Sugar: 32g

LIVER DETOX GREEN SMOOTHIE

Prep Time: 5 minutes **Cook Time:** 2 minutes **Total Time**: 7 minutes

Ingredients

- 1 cup unsweetened plant milk
- 1/2 ripe banana, frozen
- 1/3 cup frozen pineapple
- 1/4 ripe avocado
- 2 handfuls of baby spinach or baby kale
- 5–10 sprigs of fresh cilantro, stems removed

- 1/2 teaspoon ground cinnamon
- 1–2 scoops of unsweetened protein powder

Instructions

1. Fill the pitcher of your high-powered blender with milk, bananas, pineapples, avocados, spinach, cilantro, and ground cinnamon. Put in the protein powder if you're using it.
2. Put the blender on high for about 30 seconds or until everything is perfectly blended.
3. Smoothies can be served immediately or stored in the fridge for up to two days if covered.

GREEN DETOX SMOOTHIE RECIPE

Total Time: 5 minutes **Yield:** 1 glass

Ingredients

- 1 green apple
- 1 green or yellow kiwi
- 1 handful of spinach - about 50g
- ¼ squeezed lime or lemon juice
- ½ cup fruit - bananas and or pineapple, about 100 g
- 1 cup almond milk or water, coconut water - about 220 - 250 ml
- ½ cup sliced cucumber - about 50 g
- 1 small piece of fresh ginger without the skin

Instructions

1. Throw the frozen bananas and pineapple in first, then the spinach leaves, cucumber, kiwi, ginger, lime juice, apple chunks, and any other optional ingredients.
2. Mix in the chilled almond milk and continue blending for three more minutes until the mixture is completely smooth and creamy.
3. The detox smoothie should be served in a big glass or tightly covered bottle.
4. Chill and top with chia seeds for the best flavor.

BANANA COOKIES

Prep Time 15 mins **Cook Time** 30 mins **Total Time** 45 mins

Yield 30 Cookies

Ingredients

- 1 stick unsalted butter at room temperature
- 1 cup sugar
- 1 big room-temperature egg
- 1 cup mashed bananas (equivalent to around 2 1/2 large bananas)
- 1 tsp. baking soda
- 2 cups regular flour
- a pinch of salt
- 1/2 teaspoon cinnamon powder
- 1/2 teaspoon mace or crushed nutmeg
- 1/2 teaspoon clove powder
- 1 cup pecans, chopped

Instructions

1. Start preheating the oven: Turn the temperature up to 350 degrees in the oven.
2. Mix the butter and the sugar thoroughly: Combine the butter and sugar in a mixing bowl and beat until frothy. After adding the egg, continue to whisk the ingredients until they become airy and light.
3. Mix the banana and baking soda: The mashed bananas and baking soda should be combined in a separate bowl. Relax for 2 minutes. The bananas' acidity reacts with the baking soda, creating steam that puffs up the cookies.
4. Combine the banana and butter mixtures: Combine the banana and butter in a separate bowl.
5. In a separate bowl, combine the dry ingredients with a whisk. Using a whisk, combine the flour, salt, and spices. Blend in until the banana and butter combination is uniform in texture.
6. Add the mix-ins: Fold pecans or chocolate chips into the batter.
7. Drop the dough and bake the cookies: Place on a baking sheet coated with parchment paper by dropping by rounded tablespoonfuls. Wait until they are golden brown, about 11-13 minutes in the oven. Serve after cooling on wire racks.

BREAKFAST COOKIES

Prep Time: 10 minutes **Cook Time**: 16 minutes **Total Time:** 40 minutes

Yield: 12 cookies

Ingredients

- 2 cups (170 grams) of either instant oats or traditional whole-rolled oats
- 1/2 teaspoon salt
- 1 level teaspoon of cinnamon powder
- 1 cup (250g) (250g) Peanut butter, almond butter, or sunflower seed butter are other options.
- 1/4 cup (60ml) pure maple syrup
- *One-third of a cup (60 grams) of apple butter
- One large banana, mashed (about one-half cup)
- 1/2 cup of dried cranberries (75 grams total)
- 1/2 cup (70g) (70g) pepitas 1/2 cup (75g) (75g) raisins

Instructions

1. Fire up the oven to 325 degrees Fahrenheit (163 degrees Celsius). Put silicone baking mats or parchment paper on 2 big baking sheets. Putting aside.
2. Use a large bowl and a stand mixer to combine all of the ingredients. All of the ingredients should be mixed together. The dough is dense and substantial.
3. Mound 1/4 cup of cookie dough (approximately 70g per) onto the prepared baking sheet. Flatten into a cookie shape using the back of a spoon.
4. Leave in the oven for 16-19 minutes or until the edges are golden. After ten minutes, remove cookies from the baking pans to a wire rack to finish cooling.
5. Cookies can be stored for up to 5 days at room temperature or 10 days in the fridge if airtight containers are used.

Notes

1. Instructions for Freezing: Once cookies have cooled, they can be frozen for up to three months. On the counter or in the refrigerator, let the food thaw. Before serving, either bring the food up to room temperature or heat it for a few seconds in the microwave.
2. Bananas from the Freezer: You can use frozen bananas that have been thawed in this recipe. Because thawed bananas have an excessive amount of moisture, you should squeeze out as much of the remaining water as you can before mashing them. For information on how to freeze and thaw bananas for use in baking, see here.

3. Apple Butter: Although I prefer to use apple butter in these morning cookies, you may successfully substitute one-third of a cup of unsweetened applesauce for it. There is no need to make any other adjustments to the recipe.
4. A larger quantity can be made by simply doubling the amount of ingredients called for in the recipe.

BROWNIE COOKIE RECIPE

Prep Time 45 minutes **Cook Time** 13 minutes **Total Time** 58 minutes

Servings 36 cookies **Calories** 156kcal

Ingredients

- 12 ounces bittersweet chocolate chips 60-70% cacao
- 1/2 cup butter
- 3 large eggs
- 1 cup granulated sugar
- 1/4 cup brown sugar
- 1 tablespoon vanilla extract
- 1/2 teaspoon baking powder
- 1/2 teaspoon salt
- 3/4 cup all-purpose flour
- 1/4 cup unsweetened cocoa powder
- 1 cup pecans chopped, optional
- 1/2 cup mini semisweet chocolate chips

Instructions

1. Begin by melting the bittersweet chocolate chips and the butter in a large saucepan over low heat, frequently stirring to ensure a smooth and even melting process.
2. Put away from heat and forget about it.
3. Beat the eggs, sugars, vanilla, baking powder, and salt on high speed for 5 minutes, or until the batter is thick and creamy, in the bowl of a stand mixer fitted with the paddle attachment. Do not skip this step; rather, give the mixture a good 5 minutes of beating.
4. Slow the mixer down and add the melted chocolate, blending it very well.
5. Flour and cocoa powder should be stirred in until barely mixed.

6. If using, sprinkle in some chopped nuts, and stir in some little chocolate chips. Conjointly stir in to mix. The batter should now be thick like that used to make brownies.
7. Chill the batter for 30 minutes with the lid on.
8. Bring oven temperature up to 350 degrees F. Spread parchment paper out on two baking sheets.
9. Drop batter onto the prepared cookie sheets about 2 inches apart using a 1.5-tablespoon cookie scoop.
10. Toast crackers for a minute or two. Edges will be firm, but the middle will look slightly underdone when the cookie is done. The cookies will lose their crackly and fudgy qualities if you overbake them.

Nutrition

Serving: 1cookie | Calories: 156kcal | Protein: 2g | Fat: 9g | Fiber: 1g | Vitamin A: 100IU | Vitamin C: 0.1mg | Iron: 0.7mg

BASIC MUFFIN RECIPE

Yield: 12 muffins **Prep Time** 10 minutes **Cook Time** 25 minutes

Total Time 35 minutes

Ingredients

- 1/2 cup(100 g) granulated sugar 2 cups (260 g) all-purpose flour
- 2 tbsp. baking powder
- 1/2 teaspoon of salt
- 3/4 cup (180 mL) room temperature milk
- ½ cup (114 g) (114 g) melted and cooled unsalted butter
- 2 big room-temperature eggs
- 2 tbsp coarse sugar

Instructions

1. Put the oven temperature at 350 degrees Fahrenheit. Prepare a muffin tin with paper liners and set it aside.
2. Flour, sugar, baking powder, and salt should be mixed together in a separate bowl.
3. Combine the milk, butter, and eggs in a medium bowl and whisk to incorporate.
4. Then, using a silicone spatula, whisk in the flour mixture until it is just incorporated into the batter.
5. Sprinkle coarse sugar on top of the muffins once the batter has been distributed.
6. To test doneness, stick a toothpick into the center and remove it with a few moist crumbs attached. Bake for 20-25 minutes.
7. Muffins should now be cooled thoroughly on a wire rack. Even though they taste best the day they are baked, muffins can be refrigerated for a few days.

Variations

Add 1 teaspoon of vanilla essence to the blueberry muffin batter. Mix with half a cup to a cup of fresh blueberries. Strawberries in bite-size pieces and raspberries also work well.

To make cranberry orange muffins, you can substitute orange juice for a quarter cup of milk. Include a tablespoon of orange zest in the mix. Incorporate 3/4-1 cup of fresh cranberries and mix well.

Brown sugar is preferable to white sugar when baking apple cinnamon muffins. Add a pinch of ground cinnamon. Combine 3/4-1 cup of chopped apples. You can use any type of tart apple for baking.

Make lemon poppy seed muffins by substituting lemon juice for a quarter cup of milk. Add the zest of one lemon and mix well. Add 1 teaspoon of poppy seeds and mix well.

To make chocolate chip muffins, add 1 teaspoon of vanilla essence. Add in 3/4-1 cup of semisweet chocolate chips and mix well. Baking chocolate that has been coarsely chopped will also work well.

Make ahead tip

In a blender, combine the frozen bananas and pineapple pieces first, followed by the spinach leaves, cucumber, kiwi, ginger, lime juice, and apple chunks.

After mixing for a few minutes, add the almond milk and continue blending for another three minutes or until the mixture is perfectly smooth and creamy.

Third, a large glass or well-sealed bottle is ideal for serving the detox smoothie.

Put in the fridge and sprinkle some chia seeds on top for extra flavor.

CHOCOLATE MUFFINS

Prep:10 mins **Cook**:25 mins **Serves** 6

Ingredients

- 125g plain flour
- 25g cocoa powder
- 1 tsp baking powder
- 1 large egg
- 60g caster sugar
- 2 tbsp vegetable oil
- 100ml whole milk
- 50g chocolate chips
- 100g icing sugar

Instructions

1. Preheat the oven to 180 degrees Celsius (fan oven 160 degrees Fahrenheit) on gas 4. Create muffin cups by lining a muffin tin with six paper liners. Flour, cocoa, and

baking powder should be mixed together in a bigger dish using a whisk. Egg, sugar, oil, and milk should all be mixed together in a separate basin. Stir constantly while gradually pouring this mixture into the dry ingredients.

2. Depending on the size of your cake pans, bake the cakes for 20 to 25 minutes or until a toothpick inserted in the center comes out clean. If using a timer, start checking the cakes after 20 minutes. Take it out of the oven and then put it somewhere else so that it may cool down.

3. In the meantime, combine the icing sugar with 12 and 1 tablespoons of water and stir the mixture frequently until it reaches a consistency that is loose but not too liquid. After the muffins have had time to cool, the icing should be drizzled over them.

MASHED POTATO MUFFINS

Cook Time 15 mins **Calories** 82 **Serving Size** 2

Ingredients

- Potatoes
- Butter

Optional: Bacon, Cheese, Parsley, Garlic

Directions

1. Mash potatoes with butter and salt and pepper to taste, or spice them up with your favorite additions like cooked bacon, cheese, parsley, green onion, garlic, etc. Place in a muffin tin that has been greased; pierce the top with a fork and brush with melted butter or olive oil. To get a golden and crispy top, bake at 375 degrees until done.

COCONUT MUFFINS

Total Time: 30 Min. **Yield:** 8 Muffins.

Ingredients

- 2 cups all-purpose flour
- 1/2 cup sugar
- 3 teaspoons baking powder
- 1/2 teaspoon salt
- 2/3 cup milk
- 1 egg

- 1/3 cup canola oil
- 1/2 teaspoon coconut extract
- 1/4 cup sweetened shredded coconut

Topping:

- 1/4 cup sugar
- 1/4 cup sweetened shredded coconut
- 1 tablespoon butter, softened
- 1/2 teaspoon ground cinnamon

Instructions

Whisk together the flour, sugar, baking powder, and salt in a large bowl. Blend the milk, egg, oil, and extract in a separate container. Blend wet components by stirring them into dry ones. Mix in the coconut. Two-thirds fill muffin tins that have been oiled or lined with paper.

Stir together the topping ingredients and sprinkle them on top of the batter. To test doneness, insert a toothpick and bake at 400 degrees for 18-20 minutes. Let the pan cool for 5 minutes before transferring to wire rack. Serve hot.

OMELET MUFFINS

Servings: 12 muffins **Prep Time:** 10 minutes **Cook Time:** 20 minutes

Total Time: 30 minutes

Ingredients

- 8 large eggs
- 1/2 cup milk I use skim or low-fat, but whole milk also works
- 1 cup shredded cheddar cheese
- 1 cup bell peppers diced
- 1/2 cup baby spinach roughly chopped
- 1/4 tsp salt
- 2 scallions thinly sliced

Instructions

1. Set oven temperature to 350 degrees F. Prepare a greased muffin tin for use.

2. Put the eggs and milk in a medium bowl. Blend ingredients together by whisking. The ingredients for the omelet, such as cheese, peppers, spinach, salt, scallions, and other toppings, should be mixed in with the egg mixture.
3. Fill the muffin cups almost to the top with the batter. There ought to be sufficient batter to make 12 muffins.
4. Wait 20–25 minutes in the oven or until the eggs are set. Upon removal from the oven, the muffins will have a lot of air trapped within them, but as they cool, they will deflate.
5. To release the muffins from the pan, loosen the perimeters with a thin spatula. Enjoy while still hot. Keep leftover muffins in the freezer or fridge.

Notes

Make sure to oil a nonstick muffin tin before adding the batter. The egg muffins tend to stick, but if you grease a nonstick muffin tin beforehand, you should be able to easily remove them.

Shred or dice all of the omelet's fillings into tiny bits. Peppers, for instance, are best cut into 1/2-inch squares. They can now prepare meals more rapidly.

Nutrition

Serving: 1muffin, Calories: 93kcal, Carbohydrates: 1g, Protein: 7g, Sodium: 160mg, Sugar: 1g,

ZUCCHINI APPLE CARROT PANCAKES

Prep Time: 15 minutes **Cook Time:** 10 minutes **Total Time:** 25 minutes

Yield: 12 Pancakes

Ingredients

- 1 1/2 cups almond flour
- a half cup gluten-free oat flour
- 2 1/2 tsp baking powder
- 1 teaspoon ground cinnamon
- 1/2 teaspoon ground ginger
- 1/2 teaspoon ground nutmeg
- 1 teaspoon of salt
- 2 eggs
- 1-quart almond milk

- 2 teaspoon vanilla extract
- three tbsp maple syrup
- 1/2 cup shredded zucchini, with excess water, squeezed out
- 1/2 cup shredded apple, with excess water, squeezed out
- 1/2 cup shredded carrot, water squeezed out
- Cooking with coconut oil

Instructions

1. Sift together the first seven ingredients in a large basin.
2. After that, grate the zucchini, apple, and carrot. Squeeze out the excess liquid by placing on a paper towel.
3. The grated apple and vegetables should be added to the egg, almond milk, vanilla, and maple syrup mixture. Do a thorough job of combining by whisking.
4. Create a well in the center of the dry ingredients and slowly pour in the liquids, folding until just incorporated.
5. Put the batter aside for a while to chill out.
6. Coat a griddle with coconut oil and heat it over medium heat.
7. Each pancake should have around a quarter cup of batter. Prepare one side for 3–4 minutes before flipping and frying for another 3–4 minutes. If you look closely, you might be able to see some little bubbles indicating that it's time to flip.
8. Continue doing this until there is no more pancake batter.
9. Butter a plateful of pancakes and drizzle some maple syrup on top.
10. Take a bite out of that!
11. For a convenient on-the-go breakfast, make a big batch of pancakes and store them in the freezer.

Nutrition

Serving Size: 2 pancakes Calories: 291 Sugar: 9g Fiber: 5g Protein: 10g Cholesterol: 62mg

QUINOA PILAF WITH ALMONDS & GOJI BERRIES

Servings 4

Ingredients

- 1 1/2 cups quinoa
- 1 - 1 1/2 cups water
- pinch salt
- 1/4 cup goji berries or dried cranberries

- 1 Tbsp olive oil
- 1 red onion chopped (about 1 1/2 cups0
- 1/4 tsp cinnamon
- 1/4 tsp ground coriander
- 1/8 tsp turmeric
- 3/4 tsp ground cumin
- 6 Tbsp almonds chopped and toasted
- 1/4 - 1/2 cup chopped parsley

Instructions

1. The quinoa should be drained and washed thoroughly under running water. Combine it with the water, salt, and goji berries in the cooking pot. Bring to a boil, cover, and cook on low heat for 8-12 minutes or until the quinoa is tender and the water is absorbed. Get rid of the flame and let it sit for a while, preferably between 5 and 10 minutes.
2. The onion should be sautéed in olive oil until transparent and soft while the quinoa is cooking. For the final two minutes of cooking, add all the spices and stir constantly.
3. When the quinoa has done cooked, stir in the almonds and parsley along with the spicy onion mixture. Just give everything a good toss, so everything mixes together.

SAUSAGE, VEGETABLE, AND EGG SCRAMBLE

Prep: 12 Mins **Cook:** 30 Mins **Total:** 42 Mins **Yield:** Serves 4

Ingredients

- 2 medium Yukon gold potatoes, peeled and diced to a thickness of 1/2 inch
- Pepper and salt
- Unsalted butter, two teaspoons
- 6 ounces of 1/4-inch-thick slices of smoked sausage
- 1 1/2 cups of sliced
- mushrooms, 1 medium onion,
- 1 medium green bell pepper, seeded and chopped
- 1/4 cup full milk and six big eggs

Instructions

1. Cover the potatoes with cold water by an inch and bring them to a boil. Cook until potatoes are cooked, about 8 minutes, by bringing to a boil over high heat, then reducing to a simmer. Drain. Clean the frying pan.

2. Over medium heat, butter should be melted in the same skillet. Include sausage. For about 3 minutes, flipping and tossing occasionally, you can get a nice browning on both sides. Move to a bowl with a slotted spoon. Salt and pepper the vegetables before adding them to the skillet. For about 8 minutes over medium heat, stirring regularly, brown the mushrooms and soften the veggies.

3. In a medium bowl, beat the eggs and milk together. Simmer the veggies in the sausage and potatoes until the meat is cooked through and the potatoes are tender. While stirring frequently, add the egg mixture and simmer for about a minute or until the eggs are set but still creamy. Start serving right away.

4. Stay toasty! Put the skillet in the oven on low heat if the eggs are done before you're ready to eat.

Nutrition Facts

Per Serving: 346 calories; protein 18g; Fiber 3g; cholesterol 320mg; sodium 535mg.

HEALTHY GRANOLA

Prep Time: 5 mins **Cook Time:** 21 mins **Total Time:** 26 minutes

Yield: 8 cups

Ingredients

- 4 cups old-fashioned rolled oats
- 1 1/2 cups raw nuts and/or seeds
- 1 teaspoon fine-grain sea salt
- 1/2 teaspoon ground cinnamon
- 1/2 cup melted coconut oil or olive oil
- 1/2 cup maple syrup or honey
- 1 teaspoon vanilla extract
- 2/3 cup dried fruit, chopped if large
- Totally optional additional mix-ins: 1/2 cup chocolate chips or coconut flakes

Instructions

1. Have ready a big, rimmed baking sheet that has been lined with parchment paper and heated to 350 degrees Fahrenheit.
2. Oats, nuts and/or seeds, salt, and cinnamon should all be mixed together in a sizable bowl. Blend ingredients together by stirring.
3. The oil, maple syrup, honey, and vanilla should be added to the bowl. Coat each grain and nut with the coating by stirring the mixture thoroughly. Spread the granola evenly in the pan by pouring it in with a large spoon.
4. 21–24 minutes until brown, stirring once. As the granola cools, it will get crispier.
5. The granola needs to chill undisturbed (at least 45 minutes). Add some dried fruit for garnish. It's up to you whether you want your granola to be extremely clumpy, in which case you should break it up with your hands, or whether you'd rather just mix it around with a spoon.
6. Granola can be kept in an airtight container for up to 2 weeks at room temperature, or for up to 3 months in the freezer. Frozen, dried fruit has to defrost at room temperature for at least 5 minutes before being used.

EGG COCONUT OMELETTE

Preparation Time : 5 mins **Cooking Time :** 5 mins **Serves:** 1-2

Ingredients:

- Eggs: 2 nos
- Onion: 1/2 (medium-sized, chopped finely)
- Green chilies: 3 nos (chopped)
- Grated Coconut: 4 tbsp
- Butter: 1/2 tsp
- Pepper powder : 1/4 tsp
- Coriander leaves : 2 sprig (chopped)
- Milk : 3 tbsp

Instructions

1. Combine the eggs, milk, salt, green chilies, onion, grated coconut, and coriander leaves and beat until smooth.
2. Brush some butter over a hot pan and set it to low heat.
3. Incorporate the eggs and heat for a minute.
4. In order to fully cook the egg, you must flip it over.
5. Eat while it's hot, please.

GOJI CHIA PANCAKES

Ingredients

Dry

- 2 cups whole grain flour
- 1 tsp baking powder
- 1 tsp baking soda
- 3 Tbsp chia seeds

Wet

- 1 cup unsweetened non-dairy milk
- ½ cup goji berries
- ½ cup light coconut milk
- 2 Tbsp pure maple syrup
- 1 tsp apple cider vinegar
- 2 tsp pure vanilla extract

Instructions

1. In order to soften the goji berries, soak them in non-dairy milk (about one hour). For maximum efficiency, you can refrigerate the soaking liquid the night before.
2. In a large mixing bowl, thoroughly combine all of the dry ingredients.
3. Before you open the can of coconut milk, give it a good shake to emulsify.
4. Add the goji berries and coconut milk to the other liquids.
5. Put the liquids into the dry and mix thoroughly. In order to get the best results, the batter needs to rest for 10 minutes. The chia seeds will cause it to expand and become thicker. Add more non-dairy milk if it becomes too thick to stir. Though thick, the batter should spread on the griddle.
6. On medium heat, preheat a nonstick pan until very hot.
7. Re-stir the batter and spoon it onto the griddle using an ice cream or muffin scoop in 1/4-cup increments to minimize cleanup.
8. When done, each pancake should have a few burst bubbles on top.
9. Cook the other side for a minute or so, until it acquires some color.
10. Top with your favorite pancake toppings, whether that's maple syrup, nut butter, or something else entirely.

Cooking Tips

You can omit the coconut milk and replace it with the same amount of non-dairy milk but the result would be a firmer, denser pancake. The fat in the coconut milk softens the batter up a bit without having to use oil.

EASY PANCAKE RECIPE

Prep 05m **Cook** 30m **Makes** 16

Ingredients

- 2 eggs
- 1 3/4 cup milk
- 1 tsp vanilla essence
- 2 cups self-raising flour
- 1/3 cup caster sugar
- Butter, for frying, plus extra, to serve
- Maple syrup, to serve

Instructions

1. In a large container, beat together the eggs, milk, and vanilla. Put the flour through a sifter and into a big bowl. Toss in some sugar and mix. Dig a well in the center. Combine milk and sugar and add it. Mix with a whisk until everything is uniform.
2. Prepare a medium heat in a large, nonstick frying pan. Butter or frying oil spray the pan. Cook 2 pancakes at a time using 1/4 cup of the batter each for 2 minutes, or until bubbles begin to form on the top. To ensure thorough cooking, flip and continue cooking for another minute or two. Put on a plate. Wrap in foil and keep warm. Grease the pan with butter or oil between batches of the remaining mixture and repeat.
3. Add more butter and maple syrup if desired.

PEAR MUFFINS

Prep Time: 15 minutes **Cook Time:** 20 minutes **Total Time:** 35 minutes **Makes:** 12 muffins

Ingredients

- 2 cups all-purpose flour
- 1 tsp baking powder
- ½ tsp baking soda
- 2 tsp ground cinnamon
- 1 tsp ground ginger
- ¼ tsp salt
- ½ cup (1 stick) unsalted butter, room temperature
- ½ cup packed light brown sugar
- ⅓ cup granulated sugar

- 2 large eggs
- 2 tsp vanilla extract
- 1 cup whole milk
- 1 cup diced pear, from about 1 pear

Crumble Topping

- ⅓ cup all-purpose flour
- ¼ cup packed light brown sugar
- 1 tsp ground cinnamon
- 3 Tbsp unsalted butter, room temperature and cut into pieces

Vanilla Icing

- ½ cup confectioners' sugar
- 1 Tbsp milk
- ¼ tsp sat

Instructions

1. Put a 12-cup muffin tray in a preheated oven at 375 degrees and line it with paper liners.
2. To make the batter, combine the flour, sugar, baking powder, baking soda, cinnamon, ginger, and salt in a large basin and whisk until smooth.
3. Butter and both sugars should be creamed together for two to three minutes until light and fluffy in the bowl of a stand mixer or a large basin using a hand mixer.
4. Mix well after each addition of an egg. When you add the vanilla, make sure it's thoroughly combined.
5. Mix in half of the dry ingredients together with half of the milk. Then, being careful not to over-mix, add the remaining milk and dry ingredients and mix again until just incorporated.
6. Incorporate the pear cubes into the mix. Prepare muffins by placing about 3/4 cup of batter in each paper cup. Sprinkle the topping crumb mixture evenly over the tops of the batter.
7. A toothpick put into the center of a muffin should come out clean after about 20 minutes in the oven. Wait a few minutes for the muffins to cool in the tin, then transfer them to a cooling rack.
8. Drizzle with vanilla frosting once they have cooled completely.

Crumb Topping

1. Put the flour, sugar, and cinnamon into a small bowl and mix well.
2. Working with your fingers or a fork, work the butter into the dry ingredients until the mixture resembles gritty sand.

Vanilla Icing

Combine the confectioners' sugar, milk, and salt in a small bowl and whisk until smooth.

GRAPEFRUIT MUFFINS

Ingredients

- 2 1/2 cups all-purpose flour
- 1/4 tsp baking soda
- 1 tsp salt
- 1 3/4 tsps baking powder
- 1 cup sugar
- 1 1/2 tsps grapefruit zest plus 1/4 cup grapefruit juice
- 2 large eggs room temperature
- 1/4 cup whole milk room temperature
- 1/4 cup Grapefruit Spread
- 8 TBSPs unsalted butter melted and cooled

Instructions

1. Turn on your oven's heat to 350 degrees. Prepare a 12-cup muffin tray with paper baking cups or cupcake liners.
2. Mix the flour, baking powder, baking soda, and salt together in a large bowl. Putting aside.
3. The sugar, eggs, zest, juice, and milk should be whisked together in a medium bowl. Butter should be whisked in.
4. Mix the wet ingredients by folding them into the dry ones. Put two tablespoons of muffin batter in each muffin tin. Then, top with another tablespoon of batter and two teaspoons of Grapefruit Spread. Distribute the remaining batter evenly among the muffin tins.
5. Let it bake for 20 minutes, or until the sides are golden brown. Powdered sugar can be sprinkled on top once the cake has cooled. Keep for up to a week if sealed tightly.

APPLE MUFFINS

Prep Time: 10 mins **Cook Time:** 20 mins **Total Time:** 30 mins

Servings: 18 muffins

Ingredients

- 2 cups sugar
- 2 eggs
- 1 cup oil, either vegetable, canola, or coconut
- 1 teaspoon sea salt
- 1 teaspoon ground cinnamon
- 1 tsp. baking soda
- 1 teaspoon vanilla extract
- 3 cups regular flour
- 3 cups apples, peeled, cored, and diced (around 3 apples)
- (about 1/2 cup) brown sugar for topping

Instructions

1. Prepare a muffin tin with 18 paper liners and bake at 350 degrees for 20 minutes.
2. The sugar, eggs, oil, and vanilla extract should be creamed together in a mixer. Color of the mixture should be very light yellow.
3. Flour, baking soda, salt, and ground cinnamon should be mixed together in a separate basin. Mix dry ingredients into the creamed mixture. The consistency of the batter will be quite similar to that of cookie dough. Add the apple chunks and combine. Once the apples are included, the dough will become a little less stiff.
4. Nearly to the top, fill paper liners up to the recommended maximum capacity. Add a liberal amount of brown sugar on the top of each muffin.
5. Cook for 20 to 24 minutes at 350 degrees. Gets you 18 muffins.

Notes

Serving: 1grams, Calories: 280kcal, Carbohydrates: 39.3g, Protein: 2.7g, Fat: 13.2g,

CUCUMBER OMELETTE

Total Time: 15-30 Minutes **Serves:** 3

Ingredients

- 1 cup - coriander leaves
- 1 - chopped onion
- 2 - big cucumbers
- 1 cup - rice flour
- 2 to 3 - green chillies
- Salt as per taste
- Oil - 1 tbsp

How to Make Cucumber Omelette

1. Prepare the cucumbers by peeling them and grating them. Take out the seeds and give them lots of water.
2. Stir in some rice flour, chopped onion, green chilies, coriander leaves, and salt. Blend together and roll into tiny balls.
3. To prepare, heat oil in a nonstick tava.
4. Maintain a thalipeeth-like spread with each ball.
5. It's best to cook it on both sides.
6. Sprinkle with ketchup and dig in.

CHEESE OMELETTE RECIPE

Prep 5 minutes **Cook** 10 minutes **Total** 15 minutes

Yield 1

Ingredients

- 2 large eggs
- Pinch of salt
- 1 tablespoon butter separated
- 2 tablespoons cheddar cheese

Optional Garnish

- 1 teaspoon chives minced
- 1 tablespoon shredded cheddar cheese

Instructions

1. Separate the eggs into a basin of suitable size. The eggs should be whisked together until they are uniform in color and texture.
2. Whisk the eggs once more, this time adding a pinch of salt. Putting aside.
3. On medium heat, get ready an 8-inch nonstick frying pan. Insert a half tablespoon of butter.
4. Spread the melted butter around the pan so that it covers the entire surface. Scramble the eggs and add them to the pan.
5. Let the eggs cook in the pan until a curd forms, about 10-15 seconds. Then, using a spatula, gently lift the omelette's edge, and push the huge curds that form toward the pan's center, making room for the raw egg to cook.
6. Put some cheese on top of the omelet.
7. With a spatula, flip the omelet over after the egg is almost fully cooked and the cheese is melted (or earlier if you prefer runnier eggs). Please give the omelette another 30 seconds of cooking time.
8. Spread the remaining butter along the omelette's spine and flip it over.
9. Gently give the pan a shake to free the omelette, then tilt it upside down so the omelette can slide off onto a dish.
10. Sprinkle with a little bit of optional toppings and eat.

Nutrition Facts

Calories: 269kcal | Carbohydrates: 1g | Protein: 14g | Fat: 23g | Fiber: 0g | Sugar: 0g

MOROCCAN OLIVE OMELETTE

Servings 3 **Prep Time** 10m **Cook Time** 5m **Ready In** 15m

Ingredients

- six huge eggs
- 1 can (4 1/4 ounce) drained black olives
- 2 tbsp fresh parsley, chopped
- a half teaspoon caraway seed
- 1/2 teaspoon cumin powder
- To taste, season with salt and freshly ground black pepper.
- 1 teaspoon oil (olive oil)
- 1 tsp sweet paprika
- 1 teaspoon minced fresh tarragon

Instructions

1. Beat the eggs gently in a medium bowl.
2. Add the olives, parsley, caraway seeds, and cumin and stir. Add salt and pepper to taste.
3. Oil should be heated in a very hot, nonstick skillet.
4. After pouring the mixture into the pan and moving it around to distribute it evenly, you should leave it alone for 7 seconds before stirring it.
5. The uncooked egg can replace the cooked one if you tilt the pan and slide the cooked egg to the center with a spatula. When there is still a little bit of runny egg in the middle, fold the omelette in half and place it on a warm platter. Season with paprika and tarragon.
6. Serve immediately after slicing into two or three pieces.

Nutritional

Serving Size: 1 (243.5 g) Calories 474.5 Sugars - 1 g Protein - 36.8 g

CIABATTA PIZZA BREAD RECIPE

Prep Time 10 mins **Cook Time** 20 mins **Total Time** 30 mins

Servings 4

Ingredients

- 1 loaf ciabatta bread
- ½ cup pizza sauce
- 12-16 ounces mozzarella cheese
- 14-20 slices turkey pepperoni
- ⅛ cup sliced green bell pepper
- ⅛ cup sliced red onion

Instructions

1. To start, turn on the oven to 425 degrees.
2. Pizza sauce should be applied to sliced bread. Pizza toppings include pepperoni, cheese, and vegetables.
3. To get a golden brown crust and melting cheese, bake for 15-20 minutes.
4. Sprinkle with crushed red pepper, oregano, or basil for garnish. Slice and serve.

Notes

1. The ingredient amounts used will vary depending on the size of the bread and personal preference.

Nutrition

Calories: 538kcal | Carbohydrates: 57g | Protein: 31g | Fiber: 2g | Sugar: 3g

FIESTA SHRIMP COCKTAIL

Total Time: 20 Min. **Chilling Yield**: 6 Servings.

Ingredients

- 1 medium tomato, chopped
- 1/2 cup Italian salad dressing
- 1 pound peeled and deveined cooked medium shrimp

- 1/8 teaspoon hot pepper sauce
- 1 can (4 ounces) chopped green chiles
- 3 green onions, thinly sliced
- Romaine leaves
- 2 tablespoons minced fresh cilantro
- 2 teaspoons honey

Instructions

1. In a large bowl, whisk together the first eight ingredients. Store in the fridge, covered, for at least an hour.
2. Arrange 6 romaine leaves in a line on a cocktail tray or serving platter. Using a slotted spoon, divide the shrimp mixture between the bowls so that each gets about 1/2 cup.

GRILLED SALMON STEAKS ITALIAN-STYLE

Prep Time:5 mins **Cook Time:** 8 mins **Total Time**: 13 mins

Ingredients

- salt and pepper to taste
- 2 salmon steaks
- 1 tablespoon fresh lime juice
- 1 teaspoon crumbled dried thyme
- 1 tablespoon dried Italian seasoning
- 1 teaspoon crushed dried rosemary

Instructions

1. Lightly oil the grill grate of an outdoor grill and heat it over medium heat.
2. Italian spice, thyme, rosemary, salt, and pepper should be sprinkled on one side of each steak before cooking.
3. Place the seasoned side down of the steaks on the hot grill. The total grilling time, with one flip, should be around 8 minutes for flaky meat. When serving steak, drizzle with lime juice.

Nutrition Facts

Calories 324, Cholesterol 100mg, Sodium 179mg , Total Carbohydrate 3g , Dietary Fiber 2g, Total Sugars 0g, Protein 34g

ASIAN GREENS

Prep:15 mins **Cook:**10 mins **Serves** 4

Ingredients

- Vegetable oil
- 1 tablespoon
- Two Tablespoons of Oyster Sauce
- 350 g of a variety of Asian greens, including pak choi, choy sum, and tatsoi

Instructions

1. In a small saucepan, combine the oil, oyster sauce, and 1 tablespoon of water and whisk to combine. Keep cooking for another minute or two, until the food is glossy, and then remove from the heat.
2. Turn on the stove and bring the water to a boil so that it can hold the amount of pasta you require. Toss in the greens and cook them for 2 minutes on low heat, until they are wilted but still firm.
3. Large bulbs should be halved before being placed on a serving platter. Serve immediately with the sauce drizzled on top.

SHRIMP SCAMPI PIZZA

Total Time: 25 Minutes **Yield**: 3-4 Servings

Ingredients

- 2 tablespoons butter
- 2 tablespoons olive oil
- 1 tablespoon freshly minced garlic
- 1/4 cup white wine
- 1/2 teaspoon oregano
- 2 tablespoons lemon juice
- 1/2 pound medium shrimp, peeled and deveined
- 1 (12-inch) ready-made pizza crust (I used Boboli thin crust)
- 2 cups shredded Italian cheese blend, divided
- 1/2 teaspoon Italian seasoning
- 1/4 cup grated Parmesan cheese
- 1 tablespoon chopped fresh parsley, for garnish

Instructions

1. In order to bake successfully, it is necessary to preheat the oven to 450 degrees F.
2. Over medium heat, melt the butter and olive oil together in a pan. After about a minute of stirring often, add the garlic and let it simmer until the smell is gone.
3. Simmer for 1 minute after adding the wine, oregano, and lemon juice and stirring to incorporate.
4. Toss in the shrimp, and cook until the flesh is pink.
5. Use a slotted spoon to remove the shrimp and transfer them to a serving dish. Leave aside. Take the juice-filled pan from the stove.
6. Remove crust from oven after baking for 4 minutes.
7. Apply some of the leftover sauce from the pan (approximately a quarter cup) on the crust. Spread the shrimp out evenly over the cheese and then top with the remaining 1-1/2 cups of cheese. Scatter the remaining half cup of cheese on top of the pizza.
8. Italian seasoning should be sprinkled on evenly.
9. Bake for another 6-8 minutes, or until the cheese is melted and bubbling. Cheese and fresh parsley, if you choose, can be sprinkled over top.

THE BEST COLESLAW RECIPE

Prep Time 20 minutes **Chill Time** 1 hour **Total Time** 1 hour 20 minutes

Servings 6 servings

Ingredients

- 3 cups green cabbage finely shredded
- 2 cups purple cabbage finely shredded
- 1 cup carrot finely shredded

Dressing

- ½ cup mayonnaise/dressing
- 1 tablespoon white vinegar
- ½ tablespoon cider vinegar
- 2 teaspoons sugar
- ½ teaspoon celery seeds
- salt & pepper to taste

Instructions

1. In a bowl, mix together the ingredients for the dressing.

2. Mix with slaw vegetables like cabbage and carrots. Allow flavors to meld by chilling for at least an hour before serving.

Nutrition Information

Calories: 160, Carbohydrates: 8g, Protein: 1g, Cholesterol: 8mg, Sodium: 148mg, Potassium: 207mg, Fiber: 2g, Sugar: 5g

DIJON VINAIGRETTE

Prep Time: 5 mins **Total Time**: 5 mins **Servings**: 8 servings **Calories**: 82.5kcal

Ingredients

- 1/3 cup olive oil
- 1 tbsp lemon juice
- 1 tbsp white wine vinegar
- 2 tsp Dijon mustard
- 1 garlic clove minced
- salt and pepper

Instructions

Place everything in a large bowl and whisk it until it's just a little bit emulsified.

Nutrition

Serving: 1tbsp | Calories: 82.5kcal | Carbohydrates: 0.6g | Protein: 0.1g | Fat: 9g | Saturated Fat: 1.2g | Sodium: 30.3mg | Fiber: 0.1g | Sugar: 0.2g

COTTAGE CHEESE CASSEROLE

Prep time: 15 mins **Cook time**: 4 hours **Total time**: 4 hours 15 mins

Ingredients

- 2½ teaspoons butter
- ½ cup mushroom
- ½ cup onions
- ½ cup celery
- ½ cup zucchini
- ½ cup nopales

- 1 clove garlic
- ½ teaspoon dried marjoram
- ⅔ cup tomato paste
- 2 cups uncooked
- 1¼ cups water
- 1 teaspoon salt
- 1 teaspoon sweetener, I used ¼ tsp
- ¼ cup parsley
- 16 ounces low-fat cottage cheese
- ⅓ cup Parmesan cheese
- 1 cup shredded mozzarella, optional for an S meal
- 2 pounds browned and rinsed ground beef or Turkey, optional for an S meal

Instructions

1. In a large skillet, melt the butter and then sauté the mushrooms, onions, celery, nopales (cactus leaves), and garlic.
2. Mix the tomato paste, marjoram, water, macaroni, salt, sugar, and vegetables together.
3. Coat the bottom of your slow cooker with half of this mixture.
4. Sprinkle half of the Parmesan cheese and one cup of cottage cheese over the top. Layers, please.
5. Prepare in four hours on high heat.
6. If you have an Instant Pot, use the slow cooker mode on *normal for 2 hours.
7. After an hour in the oven at 350 degrees, I found that this was perfectly done.

Nutrition Information

Serves: 6 Serving size: 1 cup Calories: 256

EASY TAPENADE

Prep Time: 10 minutes **Total Time:** 10 minutes **Yield:** 1 1/2 cups

Ingredients

- 1 cup Castelvetrano olives, pitted
- 1/2 cup Niçoise or Kalamata olives, pitted
- 1/4 cup lightly packed fresh flat-leaf parsley
- 1 tablespoon drained capers
- 1/4 cup extra virgin olive oil
- 2 medium cloves garlic, pressed or minced

- 1 tablespoon lemon juice

Instructions

1. Place everything into your food processor's bowl (pitted olives, parsley, capers, olive oil, garlic and lemon juice). Briefly pulsate about 10 times, and then scrape down the jar's sides.
2. To get the consistency you want, pulse 5–10 more times until the ingredients are finely chopped but not pureed. Serve whatever you like. Refrigerating leftovers for up to two weeks is a good idea.

ASPARAGUS FRITTATA

Prep Time 15 mins **Cook Time** 20 mins **Total Time** 35 mins

Servings 4 servings

Ingredients

- 2 tablespoons unsalted butter
- 1/2 cup sliced shallots
- 1 pound thin spear asparagus, tough ends snapped off, spears cut diagonally into 1-inch lengths
- 6 large eggs
- 3/4 cup ricotta cheese
- 1/2 teaspoon salt
- 1 tablespoon minced fresh chives
- 1/4 teaspoon dried tarragon
- 1 cup shredded Gruyere or Swiss cheese

Instructions

1. To prepare shallots in butter, melt butter in a 10-inch oven-proof frying pan over medium heat.
2. Add the chopped shallots and let them simmer for about 3 minutes, stirring every so often, until they soften and become clear.
3. Cook the asparagus for 3 minutes more after adding it.
4. Combining Eggs: The eggs, ricotta cheese, and salt should be beaten together, then the chives and tarragon should be folded in.

5. The eggs should be virtually set but still runny on top, so cook them for around 4 or 5 minutes after pouring the mixture into the pan. Be sure to preheat the broiler as you cook.
6. Put cheese on top and broil it: For about 6 to 8 minutes, or until the cheese is melted and browned and the center is set, sprinkle Gruyere cheese over the eggs and broil.
7. Using oven mitts, take the pan out of the oven, and slide the frittata out onto a platter. The meat should be sliced into wedges. (The handle of the hot pan is quite dangerous. To prevent someone from touching the scorching handle when I take a pan with a long handle from the oven, I like to ice it down beforehand.

TOMATO FRITTATA

Ingredients

- 6 Servings
- 3tablespoons olive oil
- 6large eggs
- 3tablespoons finely grated Parmesan
- 1garlic clove, minced
- Sea salt and freshly ground black pepper
- 11/2 pounds ripe plum tomatoes (5–6 medium), cored, cut crosswise into 1/4' slices

Preparation

1. Have a temperature of 350 degrees in the oven ready. Prepare a medium-high flame with oil in a large, nonstick frying pan. In a medium bowl, gently whisk the eggs. Add in the cheese, garlic, salt, and pepper, and stir to combine. Pour the egg mixture into the pan after the oil has reached a shimmer, and heat until the rims of the eggs are golden brown. Cover the eggs with the tomato slices. Some of the slices might sink.
2. Put the skillet in the oven and bake the frittata for 8 to 10 minutes, or until the eggs are set in the middle. Using a heat-safe spatula, remove the frittata from the pan and place it on a serving platter. Cut into pieces and serve hot or at room temperature.

Nutrition Per Serving

Calories (kcal) 180 Dietary Fiber (g) 2 Total Sugars (g) 4 Protein (g) 9 Sodium (mg) 210

SPRING TURNIP FRITTATA

Cook time: 50 minutes **Total time:** 1 hour 10 minutes

Ingredients

- 8 ounces broccolini, trimmed
- 2 teaspoons garlic, minced
- ¼ teaspoon salt
- 1 tablespoon canola oil
- ½ cup chopped onion
- 3½ cups turnips (about 2 medium), peeled and shredded
- ¼ teaspoon salt
- 8 large eggs
- 2 large egg whites
- ¼ cup low-fat milk
- 1 tablespoon canola oil
- ½ cup shredded fontina or Cheddar cheese

Instructions

1. Have a 425 degree Fahrenheit oven ready.
2. Start boiling a lot of water. Throw in some broccoli florets, and cook until they're fork-tender, about 6-7 minutes. Good drainage. Combine in a large mixing bowl with a quarter teaspoon of salt and the minced garlic. Leave aside.
3. Place a large, oven-safe, nonstick skillet over medium heat and add the oil (1 tablespoon). Combine the turnips, onion, and 1/4 teaspoon of salt. Coat the pan with the mixture and cook for 2 minutes without stirring. Stir the mixture and scrape the bottom of the pan to incorporate any bits that have browned. Re-spread the ingredients into a flat layer and heat for another 2 minutes without stirring. Cook in a single layer for another two to four minutes, stirring every now and then, or until most of the mixture is golden brown. Slide onto a serving dish. Take out the skillet and give it a good washing.
4. Combine the whole eggs, egg whites, and milk in a mixing dish and whisk until smooth. Prepare a skillet with 1 tablespoon of oil and heat it over medium heat. Once the mixture is hot, add the egg and let it simmer for about a minute, stirring every now and then, until the egg starts to set. Put away from the stove. Cover the eggs with the turnip mixture. Cheese, then broccolini, on top.
5. Put the skillet in the oven. The frittata needs around 15 minutes in the oven to set. Take it out of the oven and wait 5 minutes before serving.

6. Using a flexible rubber spatula, loosen the frittata from the pan by sliding it along the edges, and then underneath. Prepare by slicing into wedges and serving.

SWISS CHARD FRITTATA

Prep: 10 mins **Cook**: 30 mins **Total**: 40 mins **Yield**: 6 servings **Serving Size**: 1 /6 slice

Ingredients

- 4 large eggs
- 4 large egg whites
- 1/4 cup grated Swiss Cheese
- 1/2 bunch Swish Chard, 6 1/2 cups, washed well
- 1 large white onion, sliced thin
- 2 tsp whipped butter
- kosher salt and fresh pepper, to taste

Instructions

1. The oven needs to be preheated to 400 degrees Fahrenheit.
2. Throw together eggs, egg whites, cheese, and a dash of seasoning in a mixing bowl. Leave aside.
3. Detach the chard leaves from the stalks. Make tiny dice out of the stem.
4. The leaves are rolled up and sliced into thin ribbons, about 1/8 of an inch in thickness.
5. In a ten-inch pan, melt half the butter over low heat and add the onions along with some salt and pepper.
6. Stirring occasionally, sauté the onions over low heat for 8-10 minutes, or until they have reached a translucent state.
7. Raise the heat to medium and cook until the onions get caramelized. Do not eat the onions yet.
8. Toss in the remaining butter and chard stems and turn the heat up to medium-high. The recommended time in the oven is 3–4 minutes.
9. Stir in the chard leaves and simmer for 2 to 3 minutes, or until they have wilted. Add salt and pepper to taste.
10. Turn the heat down to low and add the caramelized onions, salt, and pepper to the egg mixture in the skillet.
11. Cook over low heat for 6-8 minutes, or until the edges are firm.
12. After the base and sides have set, transfer to the oven and bake for an additional 4 to 5 minutes, or until the center is firm.

13. Take it out of the oven and invert it onto a plate by placing a dish over the pan. Prepare by slicing into wedges and serving.

GUACAMOLE SANDWICH

Prep Time 10 mins **Cook Time** 15 mins **Total Time** 25 mins

Ingredients

- 1 ripe avocado - medium to large
- ¼ to ⅓ cup finely chopped onions or 1 small to medium sized onion
- ½ to 1 teaspoon finely chopped green chilies or 1 teaspoon chopped jalapeno
- 1 garlic clove small to medium-sized, minced or finely chopped or crushed finely
- ½ teaspoon ground black pepper or ground white pepper, add as required
- 2 teaspoons olive oil - optional
- 1 to 2 tablespoons chopped coriander leaves
- ½ teaspoon lemon juice or add according to taste
- salt as required
- 8 slices white bread or brown bread or whole wheat bread

Instructions

1. Get out a cutting board and put a ripe avocado on it. Cut into the middle of the avocado and all the way around it with a knife. Take off the pit and slice the avocado in half lengthwise.
2. Use a spoon to scoop off the ripe pulp and discard the skin. Put the mashed avocado into a large bowl.
3. Mix in some chopped onions, coriander leaves, and green chiles to the avocado flesh.
4. Then, season with salt, black pepper, and a minced or finely crushed garlic clove.
5. The lemon juice should now be added according to personal preference.
6. Thoroughly combine all of the ingredients.
7. As a finishing touch, drizzle with olive oil.
8. Mash the avocado into the mixture after thoroughly mixing. Put this guacamole filling to one side.

Nutrition

Calories: 237kcal | Carbohydrates: 30g | Protein: 6g | Fiber: 5g | Sugar: 3g

LETTUCE WRAPS WITH SMOKED TROUT AND AVOCADO

Prep Time 10 minutes **Serves** 4

Ingredients

- 1 head lettuce
- 100 g Trout ribbons
- 1 avocado
- 1 apple, sliced
- 2 T Mayonnaise, to serve
- Black sesame seeds, to serve
- Pickled ginger, to serve

Instructions

1. One head of gem, cos, crisp, or any other filling-friendly, flavor-neutral lettuce.
2. Add smoked fish ribbons, avocado, apple slices, mayonnaise, black sesame seeds, and pickled ginger to the lettuce leaves, and then roll them up. Add a splash of lemon juice at the end.

CURRY SHRIMP

Total Time: 15 Min. **Yield**: 4 Servings.

Ingredients

- 1 tablespoon olive oil
- 1/4 cup finely chopped onion
- 1 pound uncooked shrimp (31-40 per pound), peeled and deveined
- 1 garlic clove, minced
- 1 teaspoon curry powder
- 1/3 cup fat-free plain Greek yogurt
- 2 tablespoons chopped fresh cilantro
- 1 tablespoon water
- 1/4 teaspoon salt
- 1/4 teaspoon pepper
- Hot cooked rice, optional

Directions

1. Start by preheating the oil in a large skillet over moderate heat. When the onion is soft, around 1-2 minutes of cooking and stirring should do the trick. Cook and stir the shrimp for 2 minutes. After you add the garlic and curry powder, stir the sauce constantly for another 30 seconds to a minute, or until the shrimp turn pink.
2. Turn off heat. Add the rest of the ingredients and stir. Cooked rice can be served alongside this dish if preferred.

EASY SALMON CROQUETTES

Prep Time 5 mins **Cook Time** 10 mins **Total Time** 15 mins **Servings** 6

Calories 110 kcal

Ingredients

- 1/2 cup Panko
- 1/4 cup flour
- 1/2 green bell pepper chopped
- 1/2 red bell pepper chopped
- (3) 5 ounce canned salmon
- 1/2 teaspoon garlic powder
- 1/2 teaspoon salt
- 1/4 teaspoon pepper
- 1 large egg lightly beaten
- 1/4 cup mayonnaise
- 1 Tablespoon Worcestershire
- 1/4 cup chopped cilantro

Instructions

1. In a bowl, combine the flour and panko. Add in some chopped bell peppers, canned salmon, garlic, salt, pepper, an egg, some mayonnaise, Worcestershire sauce, and fresh cilantro. The ingredients should be thoroughly combined.
2. Form into 6 to 8 patties, and then heat oil in a large skillet over medium heat.
3. Put the patties in the pan and cook for about 3 minutes on each side, or until they're golden brown.

Nutrition

Calories: 110kcal Carbohydrates: 9g Protein: 2g Fiber: 1g Sugar: 1g

BRUSSELS SPROUT CHIPS

Yields: 2 - 3 serving(s) **Prep Time:** 5 mins **Total Time:** 25 mins

Ingredients

- 1/2 lb. brussels sprouts, thinly sliced
- 1 tbsp. extra-virgin olive oil
- 2 tbsp. freshly grated Parmesan, plus more for garnish
- 1 tsp. garlic powder
- Kosher salt
- Freshly ground black pepper
- Caesar dressing, for dipping

Instructions

For oven

1. In order to bake, the oven needs to be heated to 400 degrees. Stir the brussels sprouts, oil, Parmesan, garlic powder, and salt & pepper in a sizable bowl. Distribute in a single layer on a baking sheet of suitable size.
2. Crisp up in the oven for 10 minutes before giving it a stir and baking for another 8 to 10 minutes. To serve, sprinkle with additional Parmesan and pass Caesar dressing on the side.

For Air Fryer

1. Stir the brussels sprouts, oil, Parmesan, garlic powder, and salt & pepper in a sizable bowl. Place in the air fryer in a single layer.
2. To achieve a crisp and golden exterior, bake at 350° for 8 minutes, toss, then bake for another 8 minutes.
3. To serve, sprinkle with additional Parmesan and pass Caesar dressing on the side.

HEALTHY BAKED CARROT CHIPS

Prep Time: 20 minutes **Cook Time:** 20 minutes **Total Time:** 40 minutes **Servings:** 8

Ingredients

- 2 pounds carrots
- 1/4 cup olive oil, or melted coconut oil
- 1 tablespoon sea salt
- 1 teaspoon ground cumin

- 1 teaspoon ground cinnamon

Instructions

1. Bake at 425 degrees Fahrenheit, preheated. Set aside several large baking sheets lined with parchment paper.
2. Remove the carrots' flowery tops. Beginning at the thick end, cut the carrots on the bias into paper-thin slices to produce long ribbons. While a chef's knife will work, a mandolin slicer set to the thinnest blade setting will produce more uniform slices. When you get to the last few, put them aside for later use in a broth or salad.
3. Combine the carrot sticks, oil, salt, cumin, and cinnamon in a big basin. Use a good, hearty toss to ensure even coating. Next, arrange the slices in a single layer on the baking sheets.
4. Toast in the oven for 12-15 minutes, or until the edges are crisp and beginning to curl. Then you should bake the chips for another 5 to 8 minutes after you flip them over to get a nice crisp on the bottoms. Once cold, store in an airtight jar for up to two weeks.

Notes

1. You can bake the chips at 325 degrees Fahrenheit for around 30 minutes without rotating them. While raw, their beauty is enhanced by a high-temperature bake.
2. The chips in the center of each pan may require an additional minute or two of cooking time, especially if your oven is older.

Serving: 1serving, Calories: 107kcal, Carbohydrates: 11g, Protein: 1g, Fat: 7g, Fiber: 3g, Sugar: 5g,

BAKED SPINACH CHIPS

Prep Time: 10 minutes **Cook Time**: 10 minutes **Total Time** 20 minutes **serves** 4

Ingredients

- 5 cups Spinach leaves
- 2 tablespoons olive oil
- 1 teaspoon ground cumin
- 1/4 teaspoon paprika
- 1/8 teaspoon cayenne pepper
- 1/4 teaspoon sea salt

Instructions

1. Set on the oven to 350 degrees F. Prepare two baking sheets by lining them with parchment paper.
2. Get a big bowl and fill it with spinach leaves. Spinach leaves should be massaged with olive oil until well coated.
3. Spread the spinach leaves out on the baking sheet so that they are not touching. Carry on until no more spinach can be found. If your spinach is particularly large, you may need to cook it on more than two oven sheets.
4. Mix together the cumin, paprika, cayenne pepper, and salt in a small bowl. Spread this seasoning over all of the spinach.
5. Stick in the oven for 8-10 minutes, keeping a close eye on them to make sure they don't burn. After 10 minutes, check for crispiness and add 1 more minute if necessary. Iterate until they reach a desired crispiness.
6. Get it out of the oven and wait until it's cold enough to touch, then dig in!

CLASSIC CHICKEN SALAD

Prep Time 15 minutes **Total Time** 15 minutes **Servings** 6 servings

Ingredients

- 2 cups cooked chicken chopped
- ½ cup mayonnaise
- 1 stalk celery chopped
- 1 green onion diced
- 1 teaspoon dijon mustard
- ½ teaspoon seasoned salt
- pepper to taste
- 1 teaspoon fresh dill optional

Instructions

1. Put everything into a little bowl and stir until fully combined.
2. To taste, season with salt and pepper.
3. Use in sandwiches or to top a salad.

Nutrition Information

Calories: 206 | Carbohydrates: 1g | Protein: 15g | Fat: 16g | Fiber: 1g | Sugar: 1g

STRAWBERRY SALAD WITH BALSAMIC

Prep Time: 10 mins **Cook Time:** 10 mins **Total Time:** 20 mins **Serves** 4

Ingredients

- ¼ cup balsamic vinegar
- 1 cup sliced strawberries
- 1 cup halved cherry tomatoes
- 1 cup halved mini mozzarella balls
- 1 ripe avocado, pitted and diced
- ⅓ cup pecans, toasted
- ⅓ cup loosely packed basil, torn
- Extra-virgin olive oil, for drizzling

- Sea salt and freshly ground black pepper

Instructions

1. The balsamic vinegar should be simmered vigorously in a small pot over medium heat. After 8 to 10 minutes of simmering on low heat, during which time the vinegar should thicken and reduce by half, give it a stir. Place in a cool place.
2. Gather the ingredients in a shallow bowl or platter: strawberries, cherry tomatoes, mozzarella, avocado, pecans, and basil. Put on some salt and pepper and a little olive oil. Throw it around carefully. Last, you should drizzle the meal with balsamic vinegar that has been reduced in size.

BEET SALAD WITH GOAT CHEESE AND BALSAMIC

Prep Time: 15 mins **Cook Time**: 1 hr **Serves** 4

Ingredients

- 4 to 5 medium beets
- Extra-virgin olive oil, for drizzling
- 2 cups salad greens, arugula or spring mix
- ½ shallot, thinly sliced
- ½ green apple, thinly sliced
- ¼ cup toasted walnuts
- 2 ounces goat cheese, torn
- Microgreens, optional
- Balsamic Vinaigrette
- Flaky sea salt
- Freshly ground black pepper

Instructions

1. At start, turn on the oven to 400 degrees Fahrenheit.
2. To prepare the beets, wrap them individually in aluminum foil and season with olive oil, salt, and pepper. Roast the beets for 40 to 90 minutes, or until they are mushy and easily pierced with a fork. The beets' size and freshness will determine how long they need to cook. After roasting the beets, take them out of the oven, discard the foil, and let them cool. As soon as they are cold to the touch, pull off the skins. When I peel an avocado, I like to hold it under a running faucet and slide the skin off with my hands.
3. Be sure to put the beets in the fridge to cool down before using them.

4. The beets should be cut into rounds about a quarter of an inch in thickness. Place the greens, shallots, apples, beets, walnuts, cheese, and micro greens (if using) into a salad bowl and mix well. Vinaigrette with balsamic vinegar can be used as a finishing touch. Add some coarse sea salt and freshly ground pepper before serving.

MEXICAN TACO SLAW

Prep Time: 15 minutes **Total Time:** 15 minutes **Yield:** 8 **Calories**: 28kcal

Ingredients

- 2 cups green cabbage, finely sliced
- 2 cups red cabbage , finely sliced

Cilantro Lime Dressing

- 3 tablespoon avocado oil
- 3 tablespoon red wine vinegar
- 1 tablespoon lime juice
- ½ teaspoon cumin
- ½ teaspoon coriander
- ½ teaspoon crushed red pepper
- ½ teaspoon dried oregano
- 1 teaspoon sea salt
- ¼ teaspoon black pepper
- ½ bunch fresh cilantro, minced
- 4 green onions, sliced

Instructions

1. Combine everything in a bowl and stir to combine.
2. Toss thoroughly to coat.
3. Put it in a sealed container away from the air.

Notes

The Dressing Typically, I don't make the dressing on the side. I simply combine all of the ingredients and toss them with the cabbage.

The dressing can be made in advance and kept in the refrigerator or an airtight container until it is needed.

Recipe Variations

1. A tangy and creamy topping for fish tacos. Mix in some mayonnaise and some crema Mexicana (or sour cream) at a ratio of 1:1. Use anywhere from 2 tablespoons to a quarter cup of mayonnaise and crème fraiche, depending on how creamy you prefer it.
2. Cabbage slaw used in Korean tacos. Add in few shredded carrots, cucumber slices, and green onions. A combination of soy sauce and sriracha may be used as a dressing. Personally, I enjoy a lot more sriracha, but feel free to tweak the amount to suit your taste.
3. Peanut-based Asian slaw dressing. Add a spoonful of peanut butter and all the extras you used to make the Korean taco slaw. I suggest using a bowl to make sure that the peanut butter is well mixed into the dressing.

Nutrition

Serving: 0.25 cup Calories: 28kcal Carbohydrates: 3g Protein: 1g Fat: 2g Saturated Fat: 1g Fiber: 1g Sugar: 1g

TEX MEX PASTA SALAD

Prep 05m **Cook** 05m **Servings** 4

Ingredients

- 320g carton cherry tomato medley mix
- 1 avocado
- 3 mini flour tortillas
- 3 green shallots
- 250g dried elbow pasta
- Canola oil, to shallow-fry
- 400g can corn kernels, rinsed, drained
- 400g can black beans, rinsed, drained
- 310g jar roasted pepper strips, drained
- 1 bunch fresh coriander
- Light sour cream, to serve

Instructions

1. Activate the water heater. Put one third of the water in a big saucepan over high heat. Keep the lid on and heat until boiling.

2. As the water boils, you can prepare the ingredients by slicing the avocado, tomato halves, and tortillas. Shallots should be thinly sliced.
3. Warm the pan further by adding the boiling water from the kettle. Put the lid back on and bring it back up to a boil. Cook the pasta for 2 minutes shorter than the time recommended on the package. Drain.
4. While the pasta is cooking, fill a frying pan with oil until it reaches within a centimeter of the rim of the pan. Warm up in a moderate oven. Cook the tortilla strips for a minute or two, or until they are golden. Place on a paper towel-lined plate to absorb excess liquid.
5. Toss the pasta with the tomato sauce, corn, beans, and peppers in a large serving bowl. Coriander leaves should be roughly chopped. Include in dish. Turn over and over again until everything is evenly distributed. To serve, layer mashed avocado, tortilla strips, and sour cream. Toss with seasonings and serve.

GREEK SALAD

Prep Time 15 mins **Total Time** 15 mins **Servings:** 4 people

Calories: 305kcal

Ingredients
For The Dressing:

- ¼ cup olive oil
- 2 tablespoons red wine vinegar
- 1 teaspoon minced garlic
- 2 teaspoons dried oregano
- 1/4 teaspoon salt

For The Salad:

- 1 large cucumber , halved lengthways and sliced
- 4 vine ripened tomatoes , cut into wedges
- 1 green pepper (capsicum), deseeded and sliced
- ½ red onion , sliced thinly
- 7 oz | 200 g good quality creamy feta cheese , cubed
- ½ cup (3 oz | 80 g) pitted Kalamata olives
- 1 large avocado , diced

Instructions

1. Combine all of the dressing ingredients in a jar or jug and whisk to combine.

2. Combine the salad ingredients in a large bowl. Blend Dressing Into It and Toss. Add more salt if it seems necessary. Serve with an Additional Dose of Oregano. Whether you're craving chicken, fish, lamb, or beef, the possibilities are endless when it comes to pairings.

Nutrition

Calories: 305kcal | Carbohydrates: 12g | Protein: 10g | Cholesterol: 44mg | Fiber: 6g | Sugar: 8g

ANTIPASTO, BOCCONCINI AND RISONI SALAD

Prep 10m **Cook** 15m **Serving** 4

Ingredients

- 375g risoni
- 1/4 cup (60ml) extra virgin olive oil
- 2 tbsp lemon juice
- 1 bunch silverbeet, leaves only, finely shredded
- 140g pkt marinated chargrilled zucchini slices
- 1/2 cup (100g) drained roasted red pepper (capsicum) strips
- 100g cherry bocconcini, halved
- 1/2 cup (60g) pitted green olives, halved
- 1 red onion, thinly sliced
- 2 tbsp chopped thyme

Instructions

1. Until al dente, or as directed on the package, boil a big pot of water and add the risoni to it. Run some cold water over your face. Good drainage. Put in a very big basin.
2. To make the dressing, put the oil and lemon juice in a liquid measuring cup and whisk until smooth. Toss the risoni in the basin after the sauce has been added.
3. To the spaghetti, toss in some silverbeet, zucchini, capsicum, bocconcini, olive, and onion. Sprinkle with seasoning and stir to mix. Move to a serving dish. You can serve it with a thyme garnish.

JAMIE'S CRANBERRY SPINACH SALAD

Prep Time:10 mins **Cook Time:**5 mins **Total Time:** 15 mins

Ingredients

- 1 tablespoon melted butter
- ¾ cup blanched and slivered almonds
- 1 pound rinsed and ripped spinach into bite-size pieces
- 1 cup cranberries, dried

Dressing:

- ½ cup vegetable oil
- ½ cup white sugar
- ¼ cup cider vinegar
- ¼ cup white wine vinegar
- 2 tablespoons toasted sesame seeds
- 1 tablespoon poppy seeds
- 2 teaspoons minced onion
- ¼ teaspoon paprika

Instructions

1. In a medium saucepan, melt the butter over low to medium heat. Almonds can be roasted in butter by cooking and stirring them. Take it off the heat and let it cool down.
2. To get the clothes ready, put the olive oil, sugar, cider vinegar, white wine vinegar, poppy seeds, sesame seeds, minced onion, and paprika in a medium bowl and mix well.
3. In a very big bowl, mix together the spinach, toasted almonds, and cranberries. The dressing should be poured over the spinach mixture, and then tossed thoroughly.

Nutrition Facts

Calories 338 Cholesterol 4mg Sodium 58mg Total Carbohydrate 30g Dietary Fiber 4g
Total Sugars 23g Protein 5g

SPINACH AND ORZO SALAD

Prep Time: 20 mins **Additional Time**: 1 hrs **Total Time**:1 hrs 20 mins

Ingredients

- 1 (16 ounce) container uncooked orzo pasta
- 1 (10 ounce) package finely chopped baby spinach leaves
- 12 pound crumbled feta cheese
- ½ red onion, finely chopped
- a quarter cup pine nuts
- ½ tsp dried basil
- ¼ tsp ground white pepper
- ½ cup extra virgin olive oil
- 1 pound balsamic vinegar

Instructions

1. Start by bringing a large saucepan of water to a boil and lightly salting it. Orzo should be cooked for 8-10 minutes, or until al dente, then drained and cooled quickly in a bowl of cold water. In a large bowl, combine the spinach, feta, onion, pine nuts, basil, and white pepper. Mix in some balsamic vinegar and olive oil and toss. Keep cool in the fridge and serve.

Nutrition Facts

Calories 491 Cholesterol 25mg Sodium 349mg Total Carbohydrate 49g Dietary Fiber 3g Total Sugars 7g Protein 16g

TACO MEAT

Yield: 12 **Prep Time**: 10 minutes **Cook Time**: 4 hours **Total Time**: 4 hours 10 minutes
Calories: 286kcal

Ingredients

- 4 lbs brisket, or chuck roast
- 1 white onion, sliced, about 1 cup
- 3 serrano peppers
- 4 cloves garlic
- 2 tablespoon dried oregano
- 1 teaspoon cumin, or crushed red pepper

- 2 teaspoon Kosher salt
- 1 teaspoon freshly ground black pepper
- 1 cup beef broth
- 1 bottle dark Mexican beer, like Dos Equis

Instructions

1. Season the brisket with salt and pepper, then brown it in a Dutch oven over medium heat.
2. Take the brisket out of the pot. The pot needs some onions, garlic, and serrano peppers. About four to five minutes of sautéing should get the onions and garlic to a fragrant state.
3. To deglaze the pan, pour in the beer and stir to combine. Cover the brisket with the beef broth and return it to the pot. Bring the liquid to a boil, then add the spices.
4. Simmer, covered, at a low heat. A two-hour cook time is recommended.
5. When the meat is done, it should be easily shreddable and falling apart.

Notes

Instant Pot Instructions: Get the seasoned chuck roast browning in the pan. The broth and onions should be added. Manual high pressure cooking for 70 minutes. Ten to fifteen minutes of pressure relief is recommended. Take the roast out of the oven and set it on a chopping board. When shredding, use two forks.

Dutch Oven Instructions: The roast needs to be browned on the stovetop so the seasoning may penetrate evenly. Prepare a 450F oven. Throw everything in the oven together, including the onions and broth. Tent with a lid and let it simmer for half an hour. Cook for a further 3 hours to 4 hours at a temperature of 350 degrees Fahrenheit.

Slow Cooker Directions: Brown the chuck roast on all sides after seasoning it. Start by placing the onions in the slow cooker, followed by the roast and the broth. Prepare in a slow cooker for 6-8 hours on low or 4-5 hours on high.

Nutrition

Calories: 286kcal Carbohydrates: 2g Protein: 29g Fiber: 1g Calcium: 38mg Iron: 4mg

GRASS FED GROUND BEEF AND ONIONS

Prep Time: 5 minutes **Cook Time:** 10 minutes **Total Time:** 15 minutes

Calories: 302kcal **Yield:** 8

Ingredients

- 3 lbs Grass-Fed Ground Beef
- ½ White Onion, diced
- 2 tsp sea salt, Himalayan or Sea Salt
- 1 tsp black pepper

Instructions

1. Put everything onto a skillet.
2. Get it nice and browned by cooking it on medium-high heat.
3. Put in the fridge until needed.
4. For use as a foundation in your food preparations

Nutrition

Calories: 302kcal Protein: 34g Cholesterol: 110mg Sodium: 693mg Calcium: 22mg Iron: 3.8mg

---

AIR FRYER BAJA FISH TACOS

Yield: 4 tacos **Prep Time:** 10 minutes **Cook Time:** 7 minutes **Calories:** 622kcal

Ingredients

- 2 lbs Cod or Halibut

Fish Taco Breading

- ½ cup masa flour
- 2 tsp Taco Seasoning

Egg Wash

- 2 Eggs
- 2 tsp Hot Sauce, I like Cholula Brand

White Sauce

- ¼ cup Creme Fraiche, or Sour Cream

- ¼ cup Mayonnaise
- Lime juice

Cabbage Slaw

- 2 cups Cabbage, finely shredded
- 3 tbsp fresh cilantro
- Lime Juice
- sea salt
- Pepper
- 16 Corn tortillas, street taco sized

Toppings

- 1 Avocado
- 4 cholula hot sauce

Instructions

Batter the Fish

- Make the fish taco-sized. Salt and pepper the fish after it has been dried off.
- In a small bowl, combine the masa flour and taco seasoning with a few teaspoons of water.
- Throw the eggs into a separate shallow dish, give them a good whisking, and then sprinkle in some of your favorite hot sauce.
- Get a baking sheet ready. Use parchment paper to line the dish rack to make dish washing a breeze.
- Use a bowl of water to wash the fish, then dip each piece into the egg wash and then the masa flour mixture.
- Put the battered fish fillets on the baking sheet that has been covered with parchment paper.

Air fryer Instructions

- Prepare the Instant Pot by placing the stand and basket inside.
- Place the fish in the air fryer basket once it has been battered. Close the air fryer's lid and program it for 7 minutes of cooking time.
- Leave enough room between the fish so that air can circulate and crisp the fish uniformly.
- Take it out and put it away in groups.

White Sauce

- Combine the creme fraiche and mayonnaise in a bowl.
- Amounts of lime juice can be adjusted to achieve the appropriate consistency.
- Whisk in a little bit of salt.

Cabbage Slaw

- Shred the cabbage very finely and place it in a large bowl.
- The lime juice and minced cilantro should be added.
- Put in some salt and pepper and mix it all together.

Nutrition

Serving: 4tacos Calories: 622kcal Carbohydrates: 47g Protein: 58g Sugar: 2g Iron: 3mg

Made in the USA
Las Vegas, NV
06 September 2023

77168373R00077